THE CHRISTIAN PAKISTAN

PROBLEMS AND PROSPECTS

A.D. ASIMI

THE CHRISTIAN MINORITY IN PAKISTAN
Problems and Prospects

ISBN-13: 978-1-77069-005-9

Printed in Canada.

Printed by Word Alive Press
131 Cordite Road, Winnipeg, MB R3W 1S1
www.wordalivepress.ca

WORD ALIVE PRESS
Just Write!

Mixed Sources
Cert no. SW-COC-001271
© 1996 FSC

FSC

To the bonds that still bind me to Pakistan,
the land of my forefathers,
I humbly dedicate this work.

FOREWORD

Pakistan was created as a new county in 1947. This is when the British rule in India was lifted and the historic sub-continent was divided into two separate countries—a Muslim Pakistan and a Hindu India. This partitioning also resulted in the division of the small Christian community in the sub-Continent into two smaller national minorities.

Since partition, India has developed into a fairly workable democracy wherein the rights and freedoms of minorities appear to be relatively well protected. Pakistan, on the other hand, has been intent on constituting itself into an "Islamic democracy". However, it appears that, up to this point, it has not been able to decide, in precise and distinct terms, as to what extent it wants to be "Islamic" and to what extent it wants to be "democratic". In fact, most Islamists in Pakistan consider this question to be irrelevant. They maintain that Islamic values and democratic values are indistinguishable. But if this be so, the question then arises: why attach the qualifier "Islamic" to "democracy"? Wouldn't "democratic" ipso facto mean "Islamic", and vice versa? There should be no need to qualify one with the other. Further, democracy is democracy. It is neither Christian, nor Muslim, nor Hindu, nor anything else. It is simply a set of values and principles by which societies choose to constitute themselves and conduct their business.

Article 2 of the current Constitution of Pakistan reads: "Islam shall be the State Religion of Pakistan and the injunctions of Islam as laid down in the Holy Qur'an and Sunnah shall be the <u>supreme Law and source of guidance for legislation</u> to be administered through the Laws enacted by the Parliament and Provincial Assemblies <u>and for policy making by the Government</u>" (Underlining provided). Obviously, the law of the land is subject to, even pre-empted by, the "supreme Law" of the Holy Qur'an and Sunnah.

Article 2A of the Constitution spells out the Islamic ideology of Pakistan: "Wherein the Principles of Democracy, freedom, equality, tolerance, and social justice <u>as enunciated by Islam</u> shall be fully observed" (Underlining provided). In other words, all the principles for the structuring of society, as well as its governance, are to be drawn from, and must remain subject to, the dictates of Islam.

Traditionally, the *Ummah,* or the "House of Islam" permits the presence of Jewish and Christian minorities, but only if they abide by a set of confining conditions known as Umar's Pact (See Appendix A). Historically, however, the "sub-houses of Islam", i.e. individual Islamic governments, have been defining the rights and roles of the said minorities as they have seen fit to do. Thus, while the Constitution of Pakistan provides for the protection of minorities, certain laws, such as the Blasphemy Law and the Hudood Ordinances, render the Constitutional protections as nothing more than paper tigers.

THE CHRISTIAN MINORITY IN PAKISTAN

Pakistani Christians felt pretty secure until 1972 when, bowing to the demands of hard Islamists, the Government, in a high-handed nationalization scheme, appropriated most Christian owned and operated schools and colleges in the land, causing lasting fear and apprehension in the hearts of Christians of Pakistan.

Ever since the establishment of Pakistan, there have been random but continuous cases when Muslims have oppressed Christians with impunity, and have subjected them to a naked street justice. In the rural areas, or small localities, where Christians are found in very small numbers, Christians dare not enter into any kind of argument or contention with Muslims however right and justifiable may be their cause. If they do, they are bound to end up on the wrong side of the issue. If, per chance, they succeed in their pursuit of justice, their success becomes the cause of vendetta and entrapment by their Muslim neighbors for the purpose of settling the score.

Matters have worsened since the promulgation of the Blasphemy Laws in 1986. The abuse of this antiquated law by Muslim fundamentalists, and "score settlers" at large, has created an atmosphere of deep apprehension and foreboding. All a Muslim has to do is to assert that he heard or saw a Christian utter a word, do a gesture, or engage in an action in a way which may be interpreted by a Muslim to be derogatory or disparaging toward the Qur'an, Prophet Mohammed, his dynasty, his Companions, or Islam and Muslims in general and become liable for punishment ranging from imprisonment to death. Obviously, Christians in Pakistan, under the Qur'anic designation of *kafirs (disbelievers/resisters)*, live every minute of their lives under the very ominous shadow of this draconian law.

FOREWORD

After the events of 9/11, there was a rash of Muslim attacks on churches and worshipping Christian congregations, some right in the Capital city, resulting in senseless loss of human life and property. Obviously, the Christians of Pakistan were escape-goated for Western actions prompted by the events of 9/11. As luck would have it, the Government of Pakistan was able to prevent these acts from spreading too wide. However, it appears that, a deep fear continues to abide, and a deep sense of vulnerability continues to haunt Christians of Pakistan.

For some reasons, it appears that, a deep and dangerous division has arisen between the self-conscious Islamists of the world and the Western civilization. The ascendency of the liberal values, and the material progress of the West, is mistakenly confused by the relatively less developed Muslim world with the triumph of the Christian values and Christian way of life. Both, the West and Christianity, therefore, seem to be equally despised by the Muslim world. Understandably, the negativity towards Christianity and Christians is particularly high in lands where Christianity was introduced and is still linked with Western countries. One such situation is found in Pakistan.

The object of this book is to present a profile of the Christian minority in Pakistan together with some suggestions for reducing its societal "marginality". As matters stand today, there is not much that can be said about the place or role of this minority in the national affairs of Pakistan. Christians do exist, and the Muslim majority is certainly conscious of their presence in their midst. But neither the Muslim majority nor the Christian minority has, so far, taken any effective steps towards composing the two into one solid national whole. Under the circumstances, there is not much that can be said about the ultimate future of Christians in the land. Of course they will continue to exist. But what kind of existence will it be? With this question in mind, an attempt has been made to challenge the Christians of Pakistan to show sufficient practical wisdom in reducing their societal marginality. It appears that this will be possible only if they follow the path of maximum reconciliation with Islam and maximum "integration" into the Islamic milieu of the land, and carve out for themselves an appropriate role in the affairs of the nation. This task is not easy. But unfortunately Christians have no other constructive choice. The only alternative is a life of ever increasing marginality, weakness, and shrinkage.

A. D. ASIMI, PH.D.
Mississauga, Canada
January, 2010

INTRODUCTION

In the pages of this book, an attempt has been made to present a profile of the Christian minority in Pakistan—its origin, development, and present circumstances, together with an objective perspective on its future in a land with an inherent Islamic orientation. In addition, some measures have been proposed that might contribute to the abilities of this minority towards making necessary adjustments to the realities of its environment. For it is this environment in which this minority and its future generations are destined to live their lives. The question which needs must be asked is: What kind of life? Will it be a life of marginality and virtual exclusion or a life of maximum acceptance, harmony, and integration and, therefore, a life of security and general well-being? This fundamental question is the whole object of this book.

The concept of "Minority" has become quite complicated and rather difficult to define. I propose to use a simplified definition: When, in the context of a socio-political system, a religious, racial, or ethnic group has the decisive ability to affect the collective or individual life of the members of another group, the former may be referred to as a "majority" and the latter as a "minority". In other words, the core of a community's minority status lies not necessarily in the smallness of its numbers but in its ongoing vulnerability to disabling tendencies at the hands of another group that wields vastly more power. In essential terms, it is the power differential between two groups that constitutes a "minority" or a "majority". Numbers are relevant but only marginally.

There is a woefully small and weak Christian minority in Pakistan. It has virtually no history of its own, except that it has existed in the land for nearly a hundred-and-fifty years. In its pre-Christianity existence, most of its members lived a peripheral life. Many of its members still lack proper integration into their socio-cultural milieu. The liberal Muslims have an accommodative attitude toward the Christian minority, but the real degree of their "accepted-ness" among the rank and file Muslims remains nothing more than tokenism. Perhaps, the most serious handicap besetting the Christian minority, both on the collective as well as individual level is that, it is inherently bereft of social prestige. Internally, it lacks effective communal organization. The Church organization, as left behind by foreign Missions, has continued to survive though in a much weakened form. But equating Church organization with communal organization is a fallacy. In many ways, the Christian community in Pakistan is nothing more than a piece of baggage left behind by the departing British Raj and the Western Christian Missions. As this community exists today, it is lacking in social prestige, political involvement, economic strength, and is badly wanting in effective communal organization.

THE CHRISTIAN MINORITY IN PAKISTAN

Organized Christian Missions began their work towards the middle of the nineteenth century. Records show that, they met a determined resistance from the upper and the middle classes. However, the dispossessed of the masses found in the new religion a golden opportunity for their uplift, and joined up in numbers. Soon an identifiable new collectivity came into being composed mostly of those who were at the periphery of the Indian society.

There is considerable justification for suggesting that, though the British Raj and the missionary organizations were responsible for the creation of this new community, their concern for the communal development of this group was never more than skin deep. It is true that missionaries embraced them wholeheartedly but this was purely for the "Mission" purposes. Of course some individual converts received a boost in their socio-economic status but, on the whole, there was not much direct concern for an effective communal development of Christians. Similarly, the British Raj, though it did provide certain measures for the security of Christians, generally refrained from direct involvement in the communal development of Christians to the degree that they could have or should have done. Their declared policy was "religious neutrality" and, perhaps this is what made it problematic for them to appear favorable towards any one religious group, especially their co-religionists.

With the freedom of India in 1947, both the Raj and the Missions have practically disappeared from the scene, leaving behind, as part of their legacy, a small and resource-less community whose life is characterized by a number of inherent weaknesses, not the least of which is its continuing foreign connectedness. The result is that, a degree of "externality" of this community is assumed by most Muslims. This

necessarily detracts from the level of perceived belongingness of Christians in the Pakistani national milieu. To top it
all off, Christians have not been able to shed the negative
social image that was the lot of a majority of them in their
pre-conversion life. Thus it is that, the community, as a
whole, continues to suffer from a persistent "image problem".

During the Raj, the overall situation of Christians was
quite different. They were one among the several religious
communities. And though they were very small in numbers,
lacked social prestige, and played no appreciable role in the
matters of the Raj, their security, as well as their fair share of
the rights and opportunities, were as much assured as of
other communities. But, with Pakistan, the situation has
changed dramatically: An estimated 1.7% of the total population, Christians are thinly scattered throughout a population of around one hundred and seventy millions. Not only
are they numerically and economically weak, but are also
perceived, by most members of the Muslim majority, as having opted for a "foreign" and "rival" religion. Pakistan was
created to be a Muslim homeland, i.e. a country to be "
owned" by Muslims for their Muslim purposes. This fact
alone is enough to create a significantly exclusionary mind-
set of Muslims towards all non-Muslims in the land. Thus, a
cloud appears to hang over the legitimacy of non-Muslims'
right to belong.

Constitutionally, Pakistan is an Islamic Theocracy. This
immediately differentiates the national status of its citizens
into those who belong to the "state religion" and those who
belong to other, and presumably, "lesser" religions. Added
to this is the deeply embedded dominance of the age-old
feudalistic value system which continues to bless all kinds of

inequality. Thus, within a part of the Muslim society, tolerance and pluralism are counted among the lesser values of life. Added to all this is the enforcement of Shariah Law, particularly the Blasphemy Law. By their very nature, these laws, and the agencies that enforce them, weigh very heavily on the lives of non-Muslims. On top of all this is the Government's continued inability, even unwillingness, to exert its full power to safe-guard the fundamental rights and freedoms of minorities. Under the circumstances, a state of generalized sense of insecurity and subjection to injustice and inequality characterizes the lives of all non-Muslims in Pakistan.

It appears that the situation of the Christian minority has been progressively getting more worrisome with the steady rise of aggressive Islamism in Pakistan. Clearly, Christians are now facing realities that have never been part of their lives before. These new realities call for new understanding and demand new approaches to the question of their wellbeing as a small religious minority.

All minorities face problems, some more some less. Some of these problems are such that minority members can learn to live with. Others are more difficult and require constant working at, resulting in complete or partial remedies. Then there are those problems that are irresolvable. In the case of such problems, a minority has no choice but to face them with well developed defenses and the employment of containment strategies.

The central source of a minority's problems resides in the majority's negative attitudes of mind and heart toward the members of the minority, both as individuals and as a group. These attitudes are maintained as a part of majority's cultural heritage, and are passed on from generation to generation. More often than not, these attitudes translate into a negative image of the minority members in terms of their societal rank or value, accompanied by an inner conviction that minority members do not merit equality with the members of the majority and, therefore, cannot be entitled to enjoy the same rights and freedoms as are enjoyed by the majority.

The problems of religious minorities are uniquely complicated. Of all the prejudices, religious prejudice happens to be the deepest driven, and is, therefore, the hardest to purge. All religions have built-in prejudices against other religions, only the way they are expressed varies from one to the other. Evidently, religion deals with ultimate questions of being, i.e. what, why, when, and wherefore of human existence. Since every religion, however primitive or crude, holds its own answers to these questions to be the best and final, a low view of all other religions becomes natural to every religion. This low view of other religions is invariably extended to the adherents of those other religions, such that they come to be regarded as willful followers of falsehoods.

In situations where two religious communities happen to be in a majority-minority relationship, religious differences can become the cause of serious problems for the minority. Quite obviously, the dominant majority will have much greater control over the political, legal, social, and economic processes and, therefore, will have the ability to inflict all kinds of material and non-material constrictions on the minority. A minority that adopts a "defiant" attitude usually ends up inviting more and serious consequence. In such cases, the majority will usually become more determined to degrade the minority, or to cut it down to size. Thus, minorities are always caught up in a "catch twenty-two". The louder they protest their minority treatment, the stronger become the negative attitudes of the majority. On the other hand, the more "pliant" they become the greater becomes the danger of the loss of their identity and ultimate absorption into the majority.

The problems facing the Christian minority in Pakistan come from three major sources. Firstly, there is an unresolved doctrinal conflict between Islam and Christianity, including each one's claim of being the absolute final of the revealed religions. This incurable conflict keeps a quiet fire of mutual rejection always smoldering. Along with this, there are some direct Qur'anic injunctions which forbid serious bonding between Muslims and *kafirs*. [The Holy Qur'an places Christians in the ranks of *Kafirs* (Sura V, verse 17); and in several instances forbids Muslims to develop bonds of friendship with *Kafirs*]. Further, it is hard to deny that, Islam commands its believers to eliminate the ugly contaminant of *kufr* from Allah's earth, or to keep it suppressed hard where it cannot be eliminated altogether. The obvious problem here is that *kufr* and *kafirs* are inseparable. To eliminate *kufr,* one has to eliminate *kafirs* since *kufr* can exist only in *kafirs*. The civilized way of eliminating *kafirs* would, of course, be to convert them to Islam. But what about those *kafirs* who resist such conversion? In such cases, the maximum obedience to the Qur'anic command would be to render the *kafirs* as extraneous a part of society as possible. However, confusion has always existed in Muslim minds as to the Jewish and Christian *kafirs* because of a well known and dire warning by the Holy Prophet Mohammed: "He who wrongs a Jew or a Christian will have me as his accuser on Judgment Day".

Secondly, there is, in the Muslim hearts, the lingering hurt because of the Christian Crusades of the early Middle Ages, and although Muslims did succeed in paying back in kind, the Crusades appear to have left a bitter deposit on the Muslim hearts against Christians and Christianity. By the same token, the Crusades continue to negatively color Christian feelings toward Muslims just as much if not more.

The major source of problems for the Christians of Pakistan, however, resides in the religious nature of Pakistan as a national state. The Constitution sets down Islam as the State Religion, making Muslims as the "preferred" citizens, if not the only rightful or real citizens. This renders all non-Muslims without an inherent national status. The only status available to them is that which is "granted" to them by the state, or by the "true Pakistanis", the Muslims. This condition of "status dependency" reduces the non-Muslims' "natural" and "universally recognized" human rights to a matter of Muslim determination. Thus, to the extent that the non-Muslims are placed under the Islamic Law and the Islamic principles of justice, to which they, in good conscience, cannot subscribe, they are placed in an anomalous national situation.

While there is intermittent or occasional mistreatment of Christians, the potential for discriminatory application of the Law, and manipulated administration of justice, is hard to deny. The situation is made worse by the fact that Islamization of Pakistan repudiates the solemn commitments made to non-Muslims by the creator of Pakistan, the "sole spokesman", Quaid-e-Azim Mohammed Ali Jinnah. According to those commitments, Pakistan was to be a secular democracy with equal citizenship rights for all, regardless of race, religion, or ethnic differences. Religion was to have no part in the business of the state. However, in total disregard of this covenantal reality, Pakistan has been consistently moving more and more toward an Islamic order. As is well known, under the Islamic Law, non-Muslims found in the House of Islam cannot be treated as equal citizens. Their official status is none other than that of *zimmies*. (Zimmies are non-Muslims who are allowed to exist but only at the outer fringes of the *Umma*, i.e. the generalized Islamic community). As an extraneous element, they can be subjected to a set of very debasing conditions[1]. During the life of Prophet Mohammed (PBUH) zimmies were indeed well treated. Perhaps because the two zimmie communities found in the House of Islam at that time—Jews and Christians—were culturally more advanced and materially better off than most of the Muslims. Additionally, these two older faiths were commonly regarded, though not openly acknowledged, as the forebears of Islam.

Since the birth of Pakistan, two ideological forces have been contending for the right of shaping the country. One is the body of hard Islamists belonging mostly to the religious establishment. The other is a body of Muslims whose minds have been sufficiently touched by modern ways of thinking[2]. The modernists would like to see Pakistan become as much of a democracy as may be possible while keeping some of the token Islamic features intact. The hard Islamists, on the

---

[1] See Umar's Pact: Appendix A

[2] If one were to venture an estimate, one might say that, up to 40% of Pakistani Muslims are outright modernists who wish for a truly pluralistic democracy in which religion will be a personal and private concern of citizens. The rest represent different degrees and shades of Islamism: About 20% are "soft Islamists" who pragmatically adhere to secular as well as religious values. The last 40% are the "hard Islamists", who cannot see Pakistan as anything other than a model Islamic state, no matter what the cost or what the consequences.

other hand, are bent upon making Pakistan an exemplary Islamic state, i.e. as close to a medieval theocracy as may be possible in this post-modern era. For all practical purposes, the hard Islamists, even though weak at the ballots, are the most potent force in the land. Given the entire history of Pakistan, the dislodging of this force from its preeminent position in the land appears rather a remote possibility. Under the circumstances, Pakistan's religious orientation appears inevitable over the foreseeable future.

Thus far, Pakistan has had three constitutions. The last one was adopted in 1973. This constitution declares Pakistan to be an "Islamic Republic"; sets down Islam as the "State Religion"; sets forth "Islamization of society" as the "central national goal"; and mandates the establishment of far reaching mechanisms for placing the law and justice system under the injunctions of the Holy Qur'an and the Sunnah. No one can be sure if, or when, Pakistan will ever want to follow a secular ideology, or if such a development is even possible. Even if it may be supposed that Pakistan will one day turn itself into a true democracy (as opposed to mere "procedural" democracy), that day is not likely to arrive for an indeterminable number of generations yet. Islamism is wrought deep into the very conception and post-emergence history of Pakistan. Throughout its life time of six decades, the only legacy Pakistan has succeeded in building is a strident Islamism. It appears that, this legacy is not likely to be put aside easily, nor any time soon.

In constitutional democracies, rights and freedoms are clearly, firmly, and unequivocally enshrined in the constitution, and no laws may be made that are likely to contravene those rights and freedoms. But, in Pakistan, law and justice are required to be grounded in Islam, and all rights and freedoms are subject to the definitions of the Holy Qur'an and Sunnah. This places Christians (and indeed all non-Muslims) in a highly vulnerable situation. It is true that, at the moment, the impact of Shariat Law is being softened by relatively tolerant elements among Muslims, and by the watchful eyes of the international community. But these protective sources are being constantly challenged by extremely vocal forces of hard Islamists. In any event, the ultimate question for non-Muslim minorities will always be: With what rigor are the Islamic provisions of the Law, such as the Blasphemy Law and the Hudood Ordinances, applied to them, and how heavily will those laws weigh on their lives and liberties?

In the meantime, it appears wise for the Christian minority to engage in a long and hard thinking process about their future, and the future of their generations to come; and to take steps that may provide the possibility of a safer, securer, and more satisfying existence in a land which happens to be their homeland as well, if for no other reason than that countless of their generations have existed on this land from time immemorial; long before there were Islam and Muslims.

Some of the proposals made herein may not sit well with the traditionalist Christians in Pakistan. For them, let it be pointed out that, Christianity is a living religion. It is in the nature of living things to evolve according to the demands of their environment. Christianity has indeed greatly evolved in the West. Leading Christian thinkers, including prominent theologians and churchmen, such as the members of Jesus Seminar, are putting forth powerful ideas for a rethinking of Christian belief system. These ideas are receiving serious consideration from a large body of rationalist Christians around the world. It must be realized that, Institutional Church and Church theology are no longer the center of faith. They are being supplanted by the direct (not Church-mediated) teachings of an historical Jesus of Nazareth. But unfortunately most Christians in the former Mission fields are still clinging to a Church-founded and Church-taught-Christianity. Clearly, the knowledge revolution of the post-modern world is constraining Christianity toward becoming more of a religion of the head than a faith of the heart. Collectivist faith is good and, in some ways, may even be necessary. But, in this age of Individualism, what is most appropriate is a personal faith. Evading this reality cannot be in the long term best interest of Christians, particularly those Christians who live their lives in the shadow of other religious systems and other cultural complexes.

My main motivation for undertaking the present work is my natural concern for the situation of Pakistani Christian community. Once I was an active member of that community. In many ways, I am still bonded to that community. Pakistan remains the land of my origin, and the land of the lives and deaths of countless of my past generations. Having been born and brought up there, I have a spiritual bond with the soil; a bond that is hard to break. What happens in that land, or to that land, affects me deeply. An extremist, intolerant, and backward-looking Pakistan remains bereft of credibility. When, in the world media, Pakistan is listed high among the "failed states" of the world; and when senseless hatred, violence, and extremism sullies the historic image of Islam (a religion of brotherliness), my heart bleeds for my homeland.

In many ways, the Christian situation in Pakistan is still evolving. No one knows what final shape it will take in the coming years and decades. Presently, one can deal only with what is on the horizon. And what is looming very large on the horizon is this: Pakistan is, and will continue to remain a religious state and society for an un-determinable length of time. The hope for true democracy is certainly there but, to the extent that Islamism is likely to persist in the affairs of the State, all that can be said with any certainty is that, the coming of true democracy will be slow and laborious unless, of course, Pakistan experiences a leader of the Kemal Ataturk variety.

With this perspective in mind, I have offered some basic ideas for an enhanced communal existence for Christians within the Islamist environment of Pakistan. These are no silver bullets but merely ideas that may, or may not, produce the desired results. In my view, the highest challenge facing Christian minority in Pakistan is to come to a stark realization of the "real life choices" available to them. I have laid out these challenges and choices, and have suggested ways of pursuing them in the most creative ways possible. Neither shrill noises of protest and bluster nor timid silence and do-nothing capitulation will serve Christian communal interests well. Practical wisdom demands conciliatory attitudes, maximum socio-cultural integration, and firm pursuit of equality in matters of law, justice, and economic opportunity. It is very true that, some elements of the Muslim community act out of alienation towards Christianity and Christians. But it is also just as true that, there is a vast reservoir of good will and fellow feelings towards Christians among most Muslims. In many Muslim societies around the world, Christian minorities live a well integrated and fairly harmonious life with their Muslim majorities. I am sure that the same can be true in Pakistan. In fact, I firmly hold that there simply is no other way. The only alternative is a life of continued exclusion and greater and greater marginality.

TABLE OF CONTENTS

ONE
The Coming of Christianity

There are stories that tell of Christianity having been brought to the southern part of India as early as 52 A.D. by none other than St Thomas, believed to be one of the twelve disciples of Jesus of Nazareth. The proof advanced is an old grave which is said to be that of St Thomas. But who is actually buried in it, has never been established. There is no authenticated record. In 2006, Pope Benedict XVI cast serious doubt on the veracity of the South Indian tradition of St. Thomas. But when the South Indians protested, the Pope modified his statement by saying that, the story of St. Thomas in South India was simply "unverifiable".

Similarly, there is an unverifiable story that, in 780, an Armenian Christian by the name of Kahana Tomas appeared on the Malabar Coast. No one knows whether he was a priest, a merchant, or both. According to the papers of the Armenian General Benevolent Union, published for "promoting the Armenian heritage around the world", he became the nucleus from which there grew tiny Armenian Christian groups in some of the Indian cities. While there is a mention of Christians, and while the existence of one or two very old cemeteries in India point to Armenian presence in the land way back then, we simply cannot be sure how material or consequential this presence was as far as the spread of Christianity is concerned. There simply are no reliable sources of information. All that can be gathered is that, very small number of Christians from abroad, particularly from Armenia were found in ancient India. It is likely that some of them might have made India their home. And while in India, might have exercised some form of Christianity. But to assert this to mean the establishment of Christian religion at any measureable level would be too much of a stretch.

As is well known, the first recorded attempt at introducing Christianity into the sub-continent of India was made by Roman Catholic Fathers from the Portuguese enclave of Goa. This was in the late 16th and early 17th centuries. It is also well known that this attempt did not succeed. The resistance to Christianity was so great that, when in 1632, Shah Jehan invaded Hugli, he massacred four to five thousand Christians, mostly foreigners but also a handful of Indians who had nominally converted to Christianity. Three years later, the same Shah Jehan issued a Royal decree outlawing Muslim conversion to Christianity. The result was that, soon there was hardly a trace of Christianity to be found in India.

The historical re-introduction of Christianity (mainly Protestant), and the eventual emergence of a Christian minority in the sub-continent of India, is intimately linked with the British Rule (also known as the British Raj). The direct exercise of British power over India began in September of 1858. However, the British influence, as such, had begun a good century-and-a-half earlier. This is when the British

2

East India Company began its operations in the sub-continent. It is well recognized that, without the British, there might have never been Christianity or Christians in this region of the world. It is also well known that, the British, and all that their name is associated with, including Christianity, was deeply resented by the people of the sub-continent, particularly after the horrific events of the Sepoy Mutiny of 1857. From then on, the British Raj, and all that it stood for, or symbolized, was passionately denounced by Indians as corruptive, alien, and inherently anti-Indian. Under the circumstances, Christianity seen as an arm of the Raj, was equally resented and resisted by the rank and file of Indians. The declared policy of the Raj was, no doubt, religious neutrality but, given the circumstances, it was hard for Indians to believe that the Raj was not intent on imposing Christianism on them. The Raj ended in 1947, but a reminder of the Raj still exists in the form of tall-steepled churches dotted around the entire landscape, along with Christian schools, colleges, hospitals, etc., established by, or patronized by the Raj. To this must also be added the presence of a small minority of Christians who practice a Western style Christianity. Most of the non-Christian population looks upon all this as an alien legacy left behind by an alien power. They were averse to this power then, and they are averse to its legacy today. For this fundamental reason, it appears necessary for us to give a factual account of the British role in planting Christianity in the sub-continent and endowing it with a resented foreign image that has been hard for local Christianity and Christians to shed.

It was in 1578 that Queen Elizabeth gave her royal assent to Humphrey Gilbert "to take possession of all the remote and barbarous lands unoccupied by any Christian prince or people" (Ogilvy, p. 1). Building empires for the sake of Christ was the most cherished pursuit of European powers of the 16th, 17[th,] and 18th centuries. Spain, Portugal, and France had already established such empires. It was certainly this spirit which made Edward VI declare to his navigators: "The serving of Christianity must be the chief interest of such as shall make any attempt at foreign discovery, or else what is built on the foundation shall never obtain happy success or continuance" (Ogilvie, p. 7). Undoubtedly, this is the spirit that prevailed when, in 1600, the East India Company began its operations in India. But, though the standard of religious duty had been set, its pursuit in India was not so simple. In the first place, the Company was a concern of private citizens whose sole aim was the growth of trade. There was no apparent thought of territorial gains, permanent settlement, or imperial expansion. Secondly, India already had two highly developed religions, one of which pre-dated Christianity by many centuries. Nonetheless, even though the spread of Christianity found no place in Company's official plans, enough provision was made for maintaining Christian religion for the employees, and for the British army stationed in India. Chaplaincies were provided at all trading centers. The chief agent at Madras built, in Fort St. George, the first Protestant church In India in 1681. One of his contemporaries at Bombay raised funds and built what is today the famous St. Thomas Cathedral. In fact, the "unofficial" exercise of Christianity was clearly in view wherever there were British personnel.

By about the middle of the 18th century, what was once a mere Company of merchants had become a dominant political force in India. Company victories at Arcot (1751), Plassey (1757), and Baxer (1764) had put a large part of the

Indian nation under the indirect rule of the Company. Soon it became necessary for the Company to engage in the wider power play within India. Henceforth, politics began to enter every consideration before the Company.

The Company found it prudent to adopt a strict policy of non-interference in Indian religious matters. In fact, it was considered extremely dangerous to do so. In this regard, the Governor General of Bengal, the Marques of Hastings, very early in the history of Britain-India relations, made this powerful remark: "One might fire a pistol into a magazine and it may not explode, but no wise man will ever hazard the experiment" (Richter, p. 131). A chaplain, returning home from India, explained this attitude of Company officials in these words: "The opinion is held, even among the most enlightened British officials in the country that, there could be no more dangerous means of estranging the hearts of the people from the Government, and no surer way of endangering the stability of the British Rule than by attempting to meddle with religious concerns of the people, however prudently and carefully one might set to work" (Richter, p. 131). In short, the Company had definitely and resolutely adopted a policy of staying away from any kind of Christian pursuit in India.

In the meantime, however, the British people and the Parliament, who had stood behind the East India Company, began to assert their right and responsibility in the administration of the colonial territories. In many quarters, this gave rise to a review of the religious policy in India. Many proposals were initiated in favor of a direct Christian policy. But, the Company remained firm in its attitude of resistance to any such involvement, and the official door to an organized Christian campaign under the auspices of the Company, remained closed. However, any of its chaplains and other employees who, in their personal capacity, cared to undertake the spreading of the Christian message, were not seriously impeded.

Before long, the stubborn refusal of Company brass to accept any Christian responsibility became a direct challenge to the Christian conscience of the British nation. A strong feeling that the expansion of England should mean something for the expansion of Christianity began to gnaw at British hearts. Consequently, an active campaign for a Christian policy in colonial India was organized under the leadership of none other than Wilberforce. In 1793, the protagonists of the Christian policy introduced the following resolution in the Parliament: "That it is the peculiar and bounden duty of the British Legislature to promote by all just and prudent means the interest and happiness of the inhabitants of the British dominion in India; and that for these ends such measures ought to be adopted as may gradually lead to their advancement in useful knowledge, and to their religious and moral advancement" (Ogilvie, p. 17).

The four decades that followed, marked an ongoing struggle between those who advocated a policy of religious neutrality in India and those who sought a strong and open policy of alliance between Christianity and the Company rule. Thus, in 1813, when Company's Charter came up for renewal, Wilberforce found a God-given opportunity to have the diffusion of Christianity recognized as a natural sequel to colonization. No less that 815 petitions were laid on the table of the House of Commons. But the neutralists showed equal firmness in opposing the direct involvement of the Company in matters of Indian religions. This is evidenced by the following dispatch sent from India in 1847: "We have uniformly maintained the principle of abstaining from all interference with the religions of the natives of India. It is obviously essential that it should be acted upon by our servants, civilian and military ... while invested with public authority, their acts cannot be regarded as those of private individuals". (Stock, p. 252)

The Indian Mutiny of 1857 stands as perhaps the most significant event in the history of Britain-India relations, eclipsed only by the demise of Britain's will to rule and the resulting religion-based partition of the sub-continent in 1947. The British historians describe the Mutiny as a rebellion of the native soldiery. The people of the sub-continent recall it as their last armed bid to rid themselves of a foreign aggression. The reasons for the Mutiny were not the same for Hindus as they were for Muslims. Yet there was a common cause that mobilized all Indians alike; namely the racial-religious cause. While some observers have made a distinction between the religious fears and the racial alienation of Indians, it is generally true to say that, in the Indian minds the two existed as one; or as merely two sides of the same coin. They looked upon Christianity as the religion of the white race, and upon the white race as the champions of Christianity.

The course of the Mutiny was marked by utter savagery and cold-bloodedness. The spirit of extreme fear and desperation, which prevailed on both sides, shook the Empire by its very roots. The Mutiny revealed, for the first time, how deep and strong were the Indian feelings of resentment, indignation, and even hatred towards the British and their power in the land.

Of course, the Mutiny was completely crushed within less than a year. But the final issue between the two peoples was never so seriously at stake as during and after the Mutiny. While the Indians felt completely demolished by the British, the British realized, perhaps for the first time, how tenuous were the foundations of the Empire, and how deep was the alienation of the native population from the British and all that they stood for. In all this, the issue of Christianity in India revived itself with a renewed vigor. The neutralists and the Christianists both launched fresh campaigns—one, to have the Christian efforts in India finally denounced and abandoned, and the other, to have religious neutrality in India decisively condemned and replaced by an open Christian policy. "For two years a serious battle was waged in England by means of press, by public meetings, and in Parliament over the question of Christianity in India" (Richter, p. 208). The neutralists charged that the uprising had been caused by Christian intrusion upon Indian religions arousing suspicion and fear in the Indian hearts. The self-righteousness and arrogance of Christian protagonists "were said to have so keenly injured the deepest feelings of both Hindus and Mohammedans, and to have threatened so violently that which they held to be most sacred, that the rebellion was regarded as a counter blow to the dreaded Christianization of the country" (Richter, p. 206).

Christianists claimed that the tragedy of Mutiny had resulted from the irreligiousness of the British posture in India. They argued that, except for the fidelity which the truly Christian rulers were able to inspire in the native hearts, the Empire would have fallen to pieces. "The Englishmen who saved India", they said, "were the Englishmen who were not only Christian themselves, but avowed their desire to see

India evangelized" (Richter, p. 228). Mutiny, according to them, was a judgment of God sent upon the British Empire for neglecting its Christian duty. Venn's Private Journal wrote: "God has a controversy with our land, and has, therefore, visited us with this judgment" (Stock, p. 228). The Indian people, the Christianists argued, could not respect a nation which had no religious purpose, much less be ruled by it. To substantiate their contention, they cited: Two-thirds of the military stations, where the British were massacred during the Mutiny, were places where no Christian work existed. The men who suffered most at the hands of the natives were men who had shown lack of religious convictions. The most restrained Indian were those who had come in touch with Christianity. Punjab, which was most likely to rebel, remained relatively calm in all probability due to the influence of rulers who openly favored a Christian policy. The greatest measure of faithfulness had come from natives who had either been converted (indeed an insignificant number) or had heard the Christian message. Thus, they maintained that, the real lesson to be learned from the Mutiny was for the British nation to recognize her Christian duty in India.

In the meantime, the Church Missionary Society of England was preparing to take other actions. For example, a memorial, signed by some of the highest names in Britain, was submitted to the Queen, urging her to have it declared: "That the existing policy will no longer be professed or maintained; but that, as it is the belief of Your Majesty, and of this Christian nation that, the adoption of the Christian religion upon an intelligent conviction of its truth, will be an incalculable benefit to the natives of India, the countenance and aid of Government will be given to any legitimate measure for bringing that religion under their notice and investigation" (Stock, p. 243).

But on July 30, 1858, the Minister for India, announced in the House of Commons: "The Government will adhere in good faith to its ancient policy of perfect neutrality in matters affecting the religions of the people of India, and we must earnestly caution all those in authority under it, not to afford by their conduct the least color to the suspicion that that policy had undergone or will undergo any change. It is perilous for men in authority to do as individuals that which they officially disclaim" (Stock, p. 251). Thoroughly alarmed by this announcement, the Church Missionary Society sent a strong deputation to the minister, but failed to budge him from his position.

There was yet another, and even greater, set back for the protagonists of a Christian policy in India. On September 1, 1858, the Company Raj was lifted and India was placed under the direct rule of the British Crown. A declaration was soon issued by Queen Victoria setting forth British policy in India. On the matter of religion, the Queen proclaimed: "Firmly relying Ourself on the truth of Christianity, and acknowledging with gratitude the solace of religion, We disclaim alike the right and the desire to impose Our convictions on any of Our subjects. We declare Our Royal will and pleasure that none be in any way favored, none molested or disquieted by reason of their religious faith or observance, but that all alike shall enjoy the equal and impartial protection of the Law; and We do strictly charge and enjoin all those who may be in authority under Us that they abstain from all interference with the religious beliefs or worship of any of Our subjects, on pain of Our highest displeasure" (Stock, p. 253). The neutralists claimed that the Proclamation had decisively established neutralism as the religious policy in India. The Christianists, however, were not so sure. They relied more on the rumors that the queen had struck down the word "neutral" from the daft of the proclamation, and while doing so had remarked with concern: "How can a government which adheres to one religion alone be neutral. Tolerant it can, and tolerant it will be" (Mayhew, p. 187).

A last push for a direct Christian policy in the sub-continent was made in 1860. This time the Duke of Marl-borough assumed the championship of the cause. He gave notice of a motion in the House of Lords for the removal of exclusion of the Bible from the course of instruction in Government Schools and Colleges in India. Within a few days, more than 20,000 petitions in favor of the motion were sent up from all parts of Britain. On July 2, 1860, the Duke moved the resolution with a long and elaborate speech. But it all came to naught. The moment he sat down, Lord Brougham, of the Government benches, sprang to his feet, and moved the previous question. In the matter of a few minutes, the Duke's resolution was history.

This marked virtually the end of the national debate over a Christian policy for India. Neutrality was, and remained, the declared policy. However, many of the Raj officials in India continued their devotion to the cause of Christianity without appearing to defy the official policy of neutrality. In the words of Mayhew, the term neutrality began to be inter-preted as a gentle tolerance of Indian religions. So, from then on, "toleration became the badge of all the British tribe in India". The real meaning of the term 'toleration' was ex-plained by Sir John Lawrence, the first Lieutenant-Governor of Punjab thusly: "I consider that it means forbearance; that is to say, we are to bear with and not persecute mankind for their religious opinions. But this cannot mean that we would not strive by gentle means to lead those in the right way whom we see to be going wrong" (Stock, p. 250).

Richter's account of the Christian-mindedness of many Raj officials is rather striking when he says that, while respecting the interests of the Empire, they were keenly desirous of being true representatives of a Christian nation. For them, duty to country included duty to Christianity. Most of them held that, the tasks of the Empire were not dissociable from the task of Christianizing India (p. 193). Similarly, Clark (p. 45) calls them "greatest Christian heroes" and states: "They were men who never hesitated to let the success of their administration, and their own credit and position depend on the results of their Christian actions and example. ... They were willing to stand or fall and to let the Empire stand or fall on this issue".

Soon after the Indian Mutiny, Lawrence and Edwards (two of the highest officials in India) returned to England. Many public organizations held meetings to honor the Christian heroes. For example, on June 24, before a large and influential assembly, an address was presented to Lawrence, thanking him for the stand he had taken in India as a Christian statesman and ruler. The address was signed by 8,000 persons, including 23 Archbishops and Bishops, 28 peers, 71 Members of Parliament, and 300 mayors, provosts, and other prominent citizens. He chose "The Safety of a Christian Policy in India" as his topic. After surveying the events of the Mutiny, and describing how the hand of God mercifully interposed to save the Empire from falling, he exclaimed: "My friends, these things are wonderful. In them we hear the voice of God. And what says that voice? That voice says India is your charge. I am the Lord of the world. I give kingdoms as I list. I gave India into the hand of England. I did not give it solely for your benefit. I gave it for the benefit of my one hundred and eighty millions of creatures. I gave it to you that you might communicate this light and knowledge and truth to these my creatures". Continuing in the same prophetic tone, he said: "When no mortal hand could save you from the results of your own policy, I the God, whom you have offended, have come to your assistance. I have lifted you up again, and I say to you, England! once more I consign this people to your charge. I say to you that once more I put you upon your trial; and I say to you take warning from the past... It is not the language of fanaticism which says 'Christianize your policy'. It is the language of wisdom, it is the language of experience. I say that the Christian policy is the policy of hope. Stand avowedly as a Christian Government" (Stock, p. 232).

By this time, however, the Christian passions of British people had largely been muted. The dominant thinking now was that, the success of the Raj was dependent on the material and intellectual uplift of Indians through the diffusion of modern civilization and the exercise of good government (Stock, p. 95). Even rulers like Sir John Lawrence who had held that the only hope for the Raj was the diffusion of Christianity, and for Britain to stand openly as a Christian Government, were now publicly avowing that the true policy for Britain was to lead people of India to throw off their outmoded ways and enter the modern age of Western civilization. But the people of India could not distinguish between Western civilization and Christian civilization. Sir Charles Napier was so right when he said that, what the people now feared was not CONVERSION to Christianity but rather a CONTAMINATION of their entire way of life

(Stock, p. 238). Under the circumstances, most Indians could not see Christianity and Westernism as separate and apart, and regarded both as equally destructive of their age old culture and civilization.

In the meantime, however, Mission organizations had emerged as quite an operation in India. There were at least twenty-seven Mission stations all across the area now covered by Pakistan. Besides, Missions had expanded their presence through the establishment of many schools, several colleges, hospitals, orphanages, and other Christian projects. Obviously, the Missions were nongovernmental organizations. Many of them were not even British. Under the circumstances, it eminently suited the purposes of the Raj to devolve all the Christianization efforts on the Missions while retaining for itself the role of the protector of such enterprises. The only requirement made of the Missions was that, they be unobtrusive in their operations, and exercise their functions with discretion. In the words of Mayhew (p. 97), "the British Government now freed from nervous scruples about its association with the Christian faith, offered a fair field and all necessary protection and opportunities for Mission work".

The Mission era began when, on November 11, 1793, the celebrated William Carey landed in Calcutta. Some Church historians refer to it as the "dawn of modern Missions in India". Richter (p.128) has suggested that the "modern period has, as its background and setting the Anglo-Indian Empire, and extended along with it from one end of the country to the other". Consequently, as Greater Punjab[1] (now most of Pakistan) was the last part of India to be conquered by the Imperial forces, so was it the last part to be reached by the foreign Missions.

On February 13, 1855, the first missionaries of the United Presbyterian Church of America, Andrew Gordon, his wife Rebecca, and his sister Elizabeth, arrived in India. On July 30[th,] he started out for Sialkot, reaching there in early September. The British officers lost no time in securing a plot of land and constructing suitable buildings, and raising enough money for the establishment of a Mission station. By September of 1855, Gordon was well settled and ready to launch out on his Christian enterprise.

Close upon the heels of United Presbyterian Mission followed another Presbyterian Mission from Scotland. In 1856, their first missionary, Thomas Hunter set out for Indian. Early in 1857, they reached Sialkot, the city chosen to be their Mission center.

All went well for a brief period until India was suddenly engulfed by the mutiny of the Indian soldiers in the British army. The lives of all white foreigners were in grave danger. Forthwith, all missionaries were removed to the forts and other places of safety. But Hunters refused to leave their post. At last, on July 9, when the situation became hopeless, the Hunters made ready to flee to the fort. But it was too late. As they rode out in their horse carriage, they were overtaken by Hurmat Khan, alias Barak Andaz, and mercilessly cut down. Even their infant son was not spared the spear of Barak Andaz.

---

[1] "Greater Punjab" refers to the original Punjab area which extended to Peshawar in the North, to Delhi in the North-East, and down to Multan and beyond in the South-West.

The shock of Hunters' murder lasted for quite some time, but the thought of abandoning the Mission never arose in anyone's mind. From these beginnings in fiver cities of Saharanpur, Ludhiana, Lahore, Amritsar, and Sialkot, the Mission work, within thirty year or so, had steadily spread into twenty-seven other cities and towns. Thus all important parts of Greater Punjab had been brought under the Missions' influence. The overall size of the Christian operation may be judged from the following figures given in the statistical tables of Protestant Missions in India (Thaker, Spink & Co, Calcutta, 1882): There were one hundred and forty missionaries with eight hundred and fourteen local agents. There were five theological schools with eighty-six students. There were eighty-one Anglo-Vernacular schools for boys, with 956 students, in addition to ninety-one vernacular schools for boys with 2667 students. Similarly, there were 126 vernacular schools for girls with 3058 students.

However, in spite of the size of the operation, the success rate of the missionary enterprise remained limited. [Here we are proceeding on the basis of the logical assumption that the most important criterion for the success of Missions had to be the number of conversion obtained]. As we review the first three decades or more of Missions, we find that the results remained quite discouraging: In 1880, the total number of adherents in metropolitan Lahore was sixty-seven (Punjab census 1881). In Rawalpindi area, the number of converts was only twenty-seven (U.P. Mission Report, 1881). For the first twelve years, Multan area remained without a single convert (Clark, p. 103). In the first twenty-four years, Sialkot area could show only thirty-three converts (U.P. Mission Report, 1865). The Scottish missionaries started work in 1857. In 1885 they could report a native

Christian membership of one hundred and seventy (Taylor, p. 7-8). Reference to this failure is frequently found in earlier reports of Missions. For instance, in 1856, there was this report from Lahore: "It is generally with feelings of disappointment that we allude to the results of our efforts for the conversion of the heathens. It is true that little, very little, has been accomplished ...It is sad and humiliating to record year after year that our labor has been, so far as we can see, almost in vain; that, of multitudes who have heard the Gospel, only here and there an individual believes, and adheres to the good news of salvation" (A.P. Mission Report 1856). The same note of despair continued in the next year's report: "We cannot review the past year without a feeling of disappointment and sadness...There may have been an improvement in the state of feelings toward the missionary on the part of the people, but we look for fruit in the actual conversion, and without that we should never be satisfied" (Gordon, p. 211).

Gordon recalls in his memoirs how the prospect remained very bleak in the early years, so much so that the Board, back home, got completely discouraged, and in many responsible quarters there were signs of willingness to abandon the enterprise altogether. The mood of despair continued to prevail until the end of the seventies when suddenly a mass movement toward Christianity began to appear among a poor section of the population. A brief account of this movement is given below:[2]

A Hindu of a fairly good standing, brought to Gordon at Sialkot a short man, lame of one leg, quiet and modest in his manners, but with sincerity and earnestness written all over his face. His name was Ditt. He lived in village Mirali, in

---

[2] Based on the memoirs of Andrew Gordon: **Our India Mission**

Zafarwal area, and belonged to a low ranking Punjab caste. He was presented to him as one who was ready to accept Christian religion. Finding him honest in his quest, the missionary baptized him, and suggested that he remain in Sialkot until he was firmly established in his new faith. But Ditt insisted on going back to his people.

No sooner did Ditt's people learn that he had abandoned the faith of his forefathers than they became very incensed, and let it be known to him in no uncertain terms. Heaping words of abuse on him, taunting him day and night, and threatening him with violence, they finally expelled him from the caste "brotherhood", the most serious punishment for any member of a caste community in the India of that age. But Ditt held his ground, arguing that what he had done was wise and could prove beneficial to their entire fraternity across the land. His determination did not remain fruitless for long. Three months later his wife, daughter, and two of their neighbors decided to join him in the new religion. In 1874, Ditt brought four more men to the Mission House in Sialkot as prospective converts. One of them, named Kaka, later joined him in an enthusiastic search for more converts.

According to Pickett (p. 440-45), Ditt had five brothers living in the same village. The clan numbered a total of sixty souls. In due course of time, Ditt was able to bring each one of them into the Christian fold. His occupation of collecting and selling raw hides took him into many villages where people of his kind lived. He made it his business to tell them of the many advantages which were to be had in accepting Christian religion. Some listened, but most were skeptical. However, Ditt continued to speak. Gradually people began to see his point of view and, before long, began to join up.

Thus the movement began to grow from strength to strength, spreading from village to village, until "it had embraced within its benign and saving influence scores of villages and hundreds of families "(Gordon, p. 425). Year after year, the movement rolled forward, ever increasing in size and strength as it advanced. The overall growth may be judged from the growth of just one Mission, the United Presbyterian Mission (based on Gordon). From almost nothing in 1873, by 1885 it had grown to include 8 organized and 56 unorganized churches in 216 villages with a total membership of 3,245.

The movement was not confined to Ditt's area, neither to the Mission which received him. Its impact was in evidence wherever there were people from Ditt's caste brotherhood. Says Gordon (p. 428): "We cannot even assert that it (mass movement) began in that locality and spread from there into others... A widespread spirit of inquiry had been found among those poor people simultaneously in districts which were separated by considerable distances and by bridgeless rivers". The movement continued in full swing into 1894 and 1895. The cumulative result of the mass movement is summed up by Pickett in these words: "By 1900, more than half of his people [i.e. Ditt's people] in the Sialkot District had been converted, and by 1915, all but a few of his people had professed the Christian faith", an estimated number of 500,000 souls.

Soon new converts began to be organized into church congregations. A number of new church buildings were erected, and Christian schools, colleges, hospitals, orphanages, etc. were put in place throughout the country. Where only a few decades before, Christianity and Christians were an oddity, they were now an established fact of Indian life.

The Coming of Christianity

Soon it became quite apparent that, for all intents and purposes, Christianity had come to stay.

TWO
The Early Development of the Christian Community

Thus far, we have taken a brief look at how Christianity was introduced into the Indian subcontinent, and how the process of creating the Christian community was advanced by an alien Raj and the alien Missions. The present chapter gives an account of the factors which firmed up the group identity of Christians as a community among other communities in the land. The term 'development' here refers to those events and processes that provided solidification and added to the permanence of a separate reality of Christians as a distinct community in the land.

It must be noted, however, that, because of the serious disabilities of the specific section of society from which majority of Christian converts were drawn, the developmental needs of the Christian community were far too many and much too complex to be taken care of with any degree of ease or speed. The deprived background of many Christians made it very difficult for the new community to mobilize its own resources for its developmental needs. In addition, of necessity, the leadership of the community was in the hands of missionaries and their hand-picked native associates. It was natural for these two groups to view the development of Christians as primarily the development of their "Christianness". Consequently, the emphasis was almost exclusively on the development of church life. Of course there were some socio-economic benefits which naturally occurred as a bye-product of the religious development of the community. But, in terms of specifically targeted communal development, there was precious little activity.

Ditt, whose conversion is generally considered to be the starting point of the Christian mass movement, was baptized in June of 1873. According to Gordon, it was from this small beginning that the Christian movement spread form house to house and village to village, until hundreds of families and scores of villages were embraced within its influence (P. 452). This then may be taken as the point of emergence of the Christian community in the area which is now Pakistan. Considering the initial failure of Missions, the numerical growth of the new community was quite rapid. At one point (1881-91) the rate of growth ran as high as 413.6 per cent. The movement continued to spread over new areas, into new villages, and among new groups, even up to the start of the twenties of the 20th century. Thus, starting from a virtual non-existence in 1873-74, the community numbered 3,823 in 1881. In addition, there were 382 Eurasians or Anglo-Indians. By 1891, the number had risen to 19,637 (Derived from India Census 1891, vol.111, part 1, Abstract 19).

Over the next decade, the membership of the community rose to 37,695, including 2,536 Roman Catholics and

35,159 Protestants. The Anglo-Indians numbered 2,309 of whom 748 were Roman Catholics and 1,561 Protestants (derived from India Census 1992, vol, XV!!). In the decade that followed, the number rose to 163,994. In the succeeding decade, the number rose to 303,336, including 270,786 Protestants, 32,553 Roman Catholics, and 4,176 Anglo-Indians of whom 2, 856 were Protestant and 1,320 Roman Catholic. The census enumeration of native Christians in 1931 showed a community of 395,629. This community has continually grown to become at least 1.7 % of an estimated total population of 170 million today.

We now look at the institutional development of the Christian community. The term "institution", in this context, refers to such operations as schools, colleges, training centers, hospitals, and orphanages etc. The presence of these institutions has been one of the most important parts of the Christian development. For instance, in 1885, different Church organizations operated 402 institutions of various kinds and descriptions (Based on different Annual Reports of Missions). In course of time, many of these simple projects developed into standardized, and much respected, high schools, colleges and hospitals. Many of them began as first of their kind and remained so for a long time. Needless to say that these institutional services have stood out as symbols of Christian presence in the land and have brought a sense of identity to Christians, from the humblest to the highest. There is a spirit-raising feeling when they see these institutions and hear themselves saying in their hearts: these are our schools, our colleges, our hospitals, our success, our prestige, our place in the land.

As for the educational development of Christians, we know that, in their pre-conversion life, they had been deprived of any kind of education. In the Muslim era, some of the restrictions began to be relaxed, and some of the lower class people had begun to acquire a minimum of reading and writing skills. But they were few and far between. Therefore, for all practical purposes, the Christian community was, at the point of its emergence, a community of illiterates. In assessing the educational development of this community, therefore, it would not be too wrong to assume zero level of education as the starting point.

Unfortunately, the information available in census reports for 1881, 1891, and 1901 (the only sources of information for those early years) pertains to the total Christian population which included Europeans and Anglo-Indians. It has not been possible to extract meaningful data applicable to native Christian community. Once in a while, a missionary report might mention the number of Christian pupils in a given school, but the overall educational progress among Christians is not identifiable. There is one record which shows that, in 1891, the total number of persons appearing in various examinations of the Punjab University was 1175, of which there were 24 Christians (Stewart, p, 121). It is hard to figure out how many of them were native Christian. However, it is well known that the first native Christian graduating from Punjab University (perhaps from any university in India) was in 1907 (U. P. Mission Report 1908, p, 102). The measure of educational progress among Christians during the early decades of their existence as gleaned from the 1911 India Census (vol. XIV, part II, Table VIII) is as follows: Out of a total Christian population of 163,220, there were 6,364 who had become literates—an outstanding achievement by any standard.

In 1923, there were 490 Christian institutions of various descriptions. The National Christian Council Proceedings, 1923, gives the following level of educational accomplishment: 72.5 % Christians had reached primary school level; 22% high school level; 2% college level; and 3% had reached professional training level (various types). It must be concluded, that a mere few decades after its inception, a fair proportion of the Christian community had attained some degree of educational accomplishment.

When looking at the economic development of Christians, we have to take serious cognizance of the following realities: It is common knowledge that up to 80% of the community was drawn from lowest economic stratum of society. Most of them had been the traditional have-nots of the land. The eradication of such deep and age old poverty requires powerful material and organizational resources. Such resources were just not there. Lack of education and the confinement of a greater part of their membership to low occupations made it very difficult for the community to attain improved economic conditions. The Missions did what they could to improve education and to teach basic economic skills to those that were available. But they could do only so much. After all, their primary concern was with the religious development of the community and that is where most of their resources had to go. It would have been nothing short of a miracle to wipe out countless generations of poverty and ignorance in as short a period as a few decades. There were two organized inquiries into the economic conditions of Christians: one by Picket in 1929-1933, and other by Lucas and Das in 1937-38. Both related to the general area of Pasrur and Narowal. As has been mentioned above, the Christians of this area were among the first to convert. In their conditions of life, they represented a typical sample of the overall Christian population. The surveys showed that of all the earners, nearly 80% were men, 10%: women, and 10% children. The average annual income per family was 133 -139 rupees. In urban areas, at least one-third of Christians were still involved in low occupations. Here and there, a few more enterprising ones had begun to turn to new work such as seamstress/tailor, carpenter, mason, gut makers, potters, cobblers, gardeners, handyman, etc. etc. A little better than 10% had progressed to working as teachers, nurses, pastors and other Church or Mission related work. About 15% owned their own houses and the sites on which they were built. The remaining owned their house structures but the sites were the village property. Two or three-roomed houses were rare. One-room houses were the norm.

Because of the legal restrictions, people officially designated as non-agriculturists (the traditional lower castes) could not own agricultural land. A very small percentage of Christians were found to have rented small parcels of land on share-crop basis, known as *b'ta-ye system*. But there were no tenantship rights. Under this system, the renter plows, sows, irrigates, weeds, takes care of the animals, harvests, but the crops belongs to the land owner who shares a mutually agreed part of it with the share-cropper. According to Lucas and Das, almost 70% village Christians were still working as farm laborers, either under the traditional *saip system* (hired hands), or under the newer *b'ta-ye system*. Their income was very low, and relative poverty was widespread.

In 1946, at the very eve of Pakistan, E. C. Bhatti, secretary of the National Christian Council, (an economist by profession), while addressing an All India Conference on

Economic Development of the Christian Community, made the following observations: Eighty to ninety per cent of the Christian community had been drawn from the low and poverty stricken part of the population. The only means of making a living available to them were the low occupations of farm laborer in villages and sanitation work in cities. A very small number of them could be considered just above the poverty line. Some were on the poverty line. But an overwhelming majority was below the poverty line. Thus, he showed that, the Christian community which started as economically the most deprived was, at the end of the first fifty years of its life, still the most deprived and depressed in the land.

Let us now look at the organizational development of the Christian community. It will be recalled that, hundreds of Bala Shahi groups, living in hundreds of scattered villages, were one people not by virtue of their non-descript Bala-Shahi religion but by virtue of their fixed low occupational life. This low identity stuck with them even after conversion to Christianity. The only difference was that, now they had a new layer of identity, i.e. the Christian identity which now began to mix with their low occupational identity. The old occupational brotherhood was replaced by the new local congregational or Church brotherhood. Small congregations were found in many small villages. In large cities, there were often, more than one congregations. Thus, for a long time the only communal organization known to Christians was their local church organization. All communal concerns were handled through the offices of this organization.

The first nation-wide organization (though still Church based) came about in 1912. A conference was held in Calcutta under the chairmanship of Dr. J. R. Mott. Many national Christians of importance attended. After four days of deliberations, it was decided that, a national body be created called the National Missionary Council. It was further decided that, each province should have a Provincial Council of Missions as a sub-body of the National Council of Missions. In 1914, the Punjab Representative Council of Missions was established. Apparently, the primary purpose of the Council was to promote the interests of Missions and missionary organizations. It is not difficult to see that, the secular interests of the small, poor, and resource-less native Christian community were not differentiated from the interests of the missionary organizations.

In 1923, however, a forward step was taken: Under resolutions passed by the Provincial Councils, the parent body was enlarged and became the National Christian Council of India, Burma, and Ceylon. The main function of Provincial councils was to carry out the policies and programs of the National Council. But, under the Constitution, the provincial councils enjoyed a good measure of autonomy. The most important objective in the constitution was: "Through common consultation, to help to form Christian public opinion and bring it to bear on the moral and social problems of the day".

Undoubtedly, the Punjab Christian Council was founded for religious purposes but, in actual practice it was also charged with leadership in the social, political, and economic spheres of the Christian communal life. This becomes very clear when we look at the proceedings of 1924 meeting, which points to Council's involvement in such areas as industrial education, social hygiene, health and medical work, military service, narcotic traffic, Land Alienation

Act, Christian Marriage Act, and other subjects of this nature.

In the Annual Meeting of 1939, a resolution was passed to enlarge the Punjab Christian Council and to include in it the contiguous areas of Delhi, North-West Frontier Province, Sind, and Kashmir (almost all of present day Pakistan). This arrangement did not last very long as the subcontinent split into two independent countries of India and Pakistan, necessitating the formation of a separate body called the Pakistan Christian Council. This body continues to exist though in a sadly devitalized and impact-less state.

We now turn to the political development of Christians. During the British Raj, all politics in India revolved around the nationalist movement for freedom from British Imperialism. The Indian National Congress was founded in 1885/86. For two decades, the Congress remained the voice of all communities—Hindus, Muslims, Sikhs, and Christians. But the Christian involvement in the national affairs was rather thin or minimal. A few prominent Christians participated in the activities of the Congress, mostly in their individual capacity. In the first place the Christian community was so small that it had no social or political weight. In the second place, most of the Christians had been drawn from a stratum of society that had been for ever considered by the upper classes as unworthy of participation in higher concerns of society. But above all, Christians lacked leadership, both in social matters and in the political arena. Whatever communal leadership was there, was in the hands of prominent Church-men. Somehow, the "secular" horizon of these men was always dwarfed by the primacy of their religious concerns, real or assumed.

Being the largest community, Hindus naturally played the most prominent role under the Indian National Congress. The Muslims who constituted one-fifth of the population were the second most important voice in Indian politics. In 1906, Muslims separated from the Congress and formed their own political organization—All Indian Muslim League. This was done in the name of protecting the special communal rights and interests of Muslims. In 1909, the British Government granted separate electorate to Hindus, Muslims, and Sikhs. From then on, all politics in India was communal. The communal division was further sharpened when in 1919, the British granted separate electorate to three remaining small communities, namely the Depressed Classes (the Untouchables), Indian Christians, and the Anglo-Indians. For all practical purposes, this was the year that the political life of the native Christian community began. The Government of India Act of 1935 not only granted legislative autonomy to the provinces but also inaugurated representation by general elections. The first general election was held in 1937. The Punjab Christian community was given two seats in the Provincial Legislature.

The years that followed were years of great political upheaval in the land. The freedom movement was gaining ground with every new day. The British Raj appeared to be running out of breathing space. In 1940, the Muslim League passed its Lahore Resolution, setting forth, in final terms, the demand for a Muslim homeland to be sliced out of the historic land of India. In 1942, the British Parliament sent the Cripps Mission to examine the situation. The Mission held many consultations with leaders of all communities except the Indian Christians. In 1946, new elections were held. These elections were followed by violent communal riots. In

March of that year, a British Cabinet Mission was sent to India for a fresh appraisal of the situation. Once again consultations were held with leaders of different Indian communities. And once again the Indian Christians were left out of the entire process. On January 2, 1947, the Viceroy held a last conference with leaders of various communities. But, once gain, the Christian community was excluded.

From the very start, Punjab, along with its contiguous areas, had been the hot bed of Hindu-Muslim strife. Since the population was predominantly Muslim, the area had become the stronghold of the Muslim League. The orthodox Hindu Mahasaba and the Akali Dal promoted the interests of Hindus and Sikhs respectively. The Christians had no comparable political organization. In any case, being only around one per cent of the population and lacking both social prestige and economic strength, and above all being devoid of an effective communal organization, Christian were extremely limited in their capacity for the political game that was being played in the national arena. According to Sir John Cumming (p. 154), political participation requires courage of involvement, sensitivity to national development, vested interest, and organizational strength. Christians of India were sadly lacking in all four.

Understandably, Indian Christians could not but have sympathy for the British Raj. Thus, in 1920, when Hindus and Muslims were fighting hard against the inauguration of the provisions of the Act of 1919, the National Christian Council issued an appeal, saying: "We urge all inhabitants of this country, to accept with good will the recent changes in the system of government". They further pleaded with the people to judge the British Government with leniency, assuring them that the "intentions of the Crown were, indeed, honorable" (Annual Proceedings 1920, p. 31). In 1929, when the political agitation was at its highest, and when men like Gandhi were advocating civil disobedience against the British Rule, the Christian community sent a message to the King assuring him of their "deep and abiding loyalty", and praying that "he may be spared for many years yet to rule over this land". (N.C.C. Proceedings 1929, p. 4)

In 1943, The National Christian Council appointed a special committee to study the political situation in the land. The following excerpts from the report of that committee, contained in the Annual Proceedings of 1944, are monumentally significant: " If the minority is to have any 'rights' they must be granted to it by the State, as the minority is not in a position to secure them for itself. It is the essence of His (Jesus) teachings about the Church that it should not try eagerly to assert its rights or be over-anxious to safe guard its own position among men .... The Church (Christians) will claim for itself only such privileges as are available for all citizens. ....It is our conviction that Christians and Churches should support the social policies and programs of the State when these appear to be in accordance with the mind of Christ; but that the Churches should never go as far as identifying themselves with particular political parties". The report went on to say: "Communal divisions in Indian life are unhappily too well known and too deep seated to be ignored. As Christians, we deplore them. We hold that the principle of representation in legislature, services, and public institutions should be on the basis of merit and worth rather than on the basis of community. We desire to see and pledge ourselves to work for the abandonment of the present undesirable system".

I am constrained to make the following remarks on the position taken by the then Christian leadership: While the report nicely starts out by recognizing the universally established truth that no minority can ever acquire any rights and freedoms except those that may be granted to it by the dominant majority, it falters rather significantly in the tone and substance of its assertions. Apart from being too pietistic, even condescending, it completely ignored the fundamental realities of Indian life that were looming large on the political horizon. It declared to the world that Christians had no desire to pursue their rights, or to safeguard their future in the shape of things to come. That Christians were content to be treated as they might be but had no mind to align themselves with the program of any one of the major political parties. In other words, they were content to be disinterested bystanders in regard to the monumental changes that were so imminent. Alas, in all this, the Christian community had shown complete lack of foresight, and had misguidedly chosen to sideline itself as an ignorable entity. They might not have amounted to much but still they had a certain place and position in society which ought to have been asserted as forcefully as possible.

We now turn to some other events of development significance for the Christian community. The first was canals and canal colonies. Between 1849 and 1927, twelve different schemes of canal irrigation were undertaken by the Punjab Government. An enormous amount of labor was required for the completion of the schemes. By 1892, the Government was anxious to employ any number of laborers. It hardly took a hint before the poor of the Christian community seized the opportunity. The result was that, whole families left their villages and moved into shacks near the work sites. Later, many moved into the new canal colonies where the landlords needed all the possible man-power in settling the land. The canals and canal colonies provided the first opportunity for village Christians to escape from the controls and disabilities that were placed on them in their ancestral villages. In fact this was their first taste of freedom from the traditional bondage-like conditions of life.

The second development event was the arising of land-owning Christians. The vast network of irrigation canals resulted in several schemes for the creation of new farmland and new farming communities. The new land was given to the "agriculturist classes" on very liberal terms. But there was no one to think of the ordinary laboring classes, including the village Christians. However, in 1867-68, the Anglican missionaries had been successful in procuring a tract of agricultural land and had proceeded to settle a small community of Christians on it. The village was called Clark-abad, after the name of the missionary who had been instrumental in its establishment. The ownership of the land was in the name of the Church Missionary Society. Christian farmers worked it as share-croppers.

This experiment had stirred up a keen desire among village Christens to become land-owning farmers. In parts of India, particularly the present Pakistan, to be a *z'mindar*, or land-owning agriculturist, has traditionally been considered a matter of pride and social prestige Around 1899, the Government was making special effort to settle a tract of land. Village Christians were eager to profit by this situation. They began to plead with missionaries to help them acquire this land. Youngson, a Scottish Presbyterian missionary was able to persuade the officials to make a grant of 3,556 acres of that land for a small colony of Christians. Two villages sprang up on this land, known as Martin-pur and Youngson-abad. Anderson and Campbell, in their book, IN THE SHADOW OF THE HIMALAYAS, describe these villages as "a most successful laboratory experiment" for Christians (p. 85). In 1951, this was a community of 225 land-owning and 125 other families. The progress of the community was symbolized by a well-run co-educational high school; and a literacy rate of 36.6% which was twice as high as the rate among the general population. By 1953, this community had produced many military and civil officers of high rank, including a high court judge, a foreign ambassador, and two inspectors of schools (U. P. Mission Handbook 1953, p. 23). This progress rate was far above the attainments of any other village community or group in the land. The people of these villages are characterized by a spirit of independence and a vigorous trend toward social progress. This is indeed a far cry from the state in which the Christians existed prior to their conversion. In the subsequent land settlement schemes, more Christians of village background were able to acquire land allotment from the Government, mostly with the help of missionary organizations. Today, there are twenty-one such Christian communities across Pakistan.

A landmark event lending religious strength to the community has been the translation of the Psalms of David into Punjabi verse for church music. From the very beginning, traditional Western hymns proved unsuitable for local worship services. Some missionaries were able to render some of the psalms into meter and set them to common Indian tunes. But more and better translations were needed. Investigation led to the discovery that among the native clergy there was one "whose soul was full of the God-given gift of poesy". He was approached and asked to render the entire Book of Psalms into rhyme and meter. The task was stupendous, but Imamud-din Shahbaz (a Muslim convert) accepted the challenge. In his first attempt of several years, he rendered a number of Psalms into Urdu meter and fitted them with tunes of Western hymns. However, it was not until a Punjabi version of all the Psalms, fitted to the soulful Punjabi tunes, was made by Shahbaz that the ZABURS began to capture the hearts of Christians in all of Northern India. The first publication of the Book of Punjabi Zaburs was in 1908. Since then, the most used source of praise in all Christian services has been Dr. Shahbaz's versified rendition of King David's Psalms.

Was it from the strain of years of pouring over the Psalms one by one, reading them over and over again, extracting their sense, and then putting them into precise Punjabi words and phrases, or was it from other reasons, but it so happened that Shahbaz lost his eye-sight while still in the middle of his long and arduous poetic undertaking. From then on, in addition to having musicians on his team, he had young and faithful readers to assist him. They would read, in prose, a verse of a psalm from the existing Urdu translation of the Bible; Shahbaz would repeat the verse aloud a few times until a fine versified translation of it would be issuing forth from his lips. This process continued until the blinded poet had rendered all of the one hundred and fifty Psalms into Punjabi verse, and had them put to Punjabi tunes. We cannot know for sure, but looking at Shahbaz's labor of love, one is tempted to say that he scarified his eyesight for the cause of Christian Church in India. He will always be a hero to the Christian Church in Pakistan. And his memory will live for ever. He died in 1921, leaving a legacy of which the Christian community can be rightfully proud. One might say that, Punjabi Zabur is, perhaps, the only piece of indigenous Christianity to be found in the land and, therefore, the single most significant contribution to the communal life of Christians. Shahbaz's achievement was recognized as far as Tarkio College, in the State of Missouri, which conferred upon him the honorary degree of Doctor of Divinity.

Another developmental event took place in 1915. Before the First World War, lower classes were not admitted into British military service. This included Christians. But during the First World War, the pressure for man-power was so acute that the Government felt obliged to open enlistment to all. Christians who had already made many unsuccessful attempts to enter military service, were the foremost in taking advantage of the new opportunity. They poured into the recruiting centers and soon there were six thousand of them in arms, plus many more who enlisted as drivers, hospital assistants, Y.M.C.A. workers, chaplains, and ordinary laborers. For some time Christians were limited to non-combatant units. This was resented by Christians. A movement was set afoot to move the Government to change this policy. A demand for a Christian regiment was formulated and put up. At lasts the Government agreed to forming a temporary Christian Regiment as only a war measure. Entry into military service marked a major step in the development of the Christian community. It represented an acknowledgement of their right to equality of opportunity, and recognition of their status as being at par with Hindus, Muslims, and Sikhs, irrespective of their background. [NOTE: Since the making of Pakistan, military service has been wide open to Christians who have made an outstanding contribution to this aspect of national life].

Yet another developmental event took place in 1925: In 1900, the Government of India had passed the Land Alienations Act. Under this Act, the Government designated some classes as "agriculturists" and others, mostly lower classes, as "non-agriculturists". Henceforth, the agricultural land could be owned only by those who had been designated as "agriculturists". This put the traditionally landless classes under a permanent disability. Christians, who had been placed in the "non-agriculturists" category, were greatly distressed by this socio-economic handicap, particularly because some Christian villages of land-owning Christians had already been established. But the community as a whole had been barred from acquiring the status of z'meendar (agriculturists). In 1925, The Punjab Christian Council passed a resolution authorizing its Public Questions Committee to take up the issue with the Government. After a year's effort, the Committee was able to report that the Government, through its notification # 2434, dated December 1925, had declared that Christians residing in the districts of Lyallpur, Gujranwala, Sheikhupura, and Montgomery were henceforth designated as agriculturists. This was only a partial victory, yet it must be counted among the major developmental events for the Christian community.

No account of the development of the Christian community would be complete without a brief inclusion of the Sialkot Convention; a yearly communal event for the last 110 years. In 1897, six hundred and fifty Christians from all major Protestant denominations gathered in Sialkot in order to demonstrate "unity" and "strength" (U. P. Mission Report 1898, p. 87). On the grounds of a Mission property, they pitched tents, and stayed there for a week, sharing Christian experiences; socializing together, worshipping together, and generally being visible to the non-Christians of the population. The event was so successful that it has continued to be repeated, and has become a regular calendar event for the Christian community. People from far and near come to be with other Christians and to strengthen communal bonds. Dr. Garfield Williams, a foreign visitor to the Convention in 1910, made the following cogent remark: "My impression is that the greatest work done at Sialkot Convention is not deepening the spiritual life of those hundreds of village Christians, but it seems to me that the greatest work Sialkot Convention does is to make these downtrodden men and women realize themselves, and their potentialities, and expect great things of the future. This self-consciousness of the Christian community of its own possibilities and its future is certainly a very significant product of the Convention" (U. P. Mission Handbook 1910, p. 30).

Since the 1950's, other Christian communities in larger cities have started their own Conventions, patterned after the Sialkot Convention and, to a large extent, are accomplishing the same community goals that the mother of such Conventions has been accomplishing for over 110 years.

In summarizing, it may be noted that the development of the Christian community, in the first more than fifty years of its life, was certainly helped by the events and processes that have been discussed above. They contributed a sense of communal identity, and a certain degree of one-ness to Christians. But, there were still major holes in the communal development of Christians: Numerically, they were still the smallest of all communities. A certain portion of them, both in cities and towns, were still confined to low occupational life and relative poverty. The leadership of the community was in the hands of foreign missionaries or their native underlings. Naturally, the mind and the will of these leaders were fixed on the religious development of Christians. Concern for their secular development was considered secondary to their religious development. All the emphasis was on such abstract Scriptural teaching as: "Seek ye first the kingdom of God and all these things shall be added on to you". Political agitation was considered as being against the mind of Christ. Similarly, any preoccupation with secular matters was considered lack of "Christian faith". The small number of well educated in the community were steered into work required for the development of the Church— Teachers for Mission Schools and Colleges, doctors and nurses for Mission Hospitals, pastors and preachers for the conduct of Church business and the furtherance of evangelical work. Promotion of missionary aims was given precedence over other developmental considerations. The necessary result was that, the development of the Christian community was lopsided. All the focus was on Church life. The religious and spiritual concern trumped all other needs and requirements. This is not to say that, no secular development took place. Of course, there was a minimal secular development. But it was purely incidental. There were simply no actively formulated community development plans or programs.

Perhaps this phenomenon is explainable by the fact that an overwhelming majority of Christians had been gathered out of a life of relative poverty and social exclusion. They simply did not have the capacity for making big strides towards socio-economic or political development. But this begs the obvious argument that this lack of capacity for development should have become the most pressing reason for taking early steps towards building up the necessary developmental capabilities, if for no other reason then for the creation of a strong and independent indigenous Church. The net result of all this short-sightedness was that socio-cultural and political isolation became the hall mark of the Christian community. This lack of integration of Christians into the local milieu has often made their non-Christian neighbors suspicious of their national loyalties. With such suspicions, the presence of Christianity and Christians has been regarded as nothing more than an odd reality which has merely to be tolerated without real acceptance.

THREE
Christian-Muslim Relations: A Cursory Review

In any situation of Christian-Muslim relations, aside from the particular elements of the given situation, there is always a degree of unavoidable influence of the historic rift between the two religions on the shape of their relationships. These two religions have been the strangest bedfellows. They are so close and yet so apart. As Brown (p. 6ff) puts it, Islam arose in a country where Christianity was well known though not widely accepted. There is a common belief that Prophet Mohammed (PBUH) was quite familiar with the Jewish-Christian teachings of his day. Islam first spread into the countries of Syria and Egypt where, at the time, Christianity was the dominant religion. Thus, from the very beginning, there was eminent prospect for the adherents of the two religions to know and understand each other. Instead, a formidable wall of misunderstanding and alienation has continued to exist between the two. The blame for this deep gulf is most commonly put upon the Crusades.

Nothing, it seems, has done more to perpetuate this estrangement than the mutual mistrust and hatred resulting from the long years of fighting and killing during the Crusades. According to Herrick (p. 37), "for hundreds of years that hatred has, among all Musallman people, been kept aflame as a sacred duty, a legacy, a heritage, from father to son". By the same token, a similar legacy of estrangement has been religiously handed down to every succeeding generation of Christians. A blind spot against Islam and Muslims has always existed in the recesses of the Christian mind. The Christian ideas of, and attitudes towards, Islam and Muslims have been much less charitable than what Christians have usually been able to confess. In 1913, Speer, a lifetime missionary in India, while addressing a conference of Americans and Canadians on the Muslim question, made this admission: "We do not remove in one generation feelings that have been wrought into the temper of Christendom for twelve hundred years ... We have never got away from the temper of the Crusades" (p. 122). Christians have consistently derided Islam in terms such as: "Its philosophy is crude, its ideals are low, and its authoritative revelation is a hindrance to progress" (Pratt, p. 451). In short, Christian-Muslim estrangement is an age old problem and, in spite of having many things in common, the peoples of the two faiths have remained in rival camps ever since their early days (Levonian, p. 9).

During the Middle Ages, the greatest power in the Middle East and Central Asia were the Mongols. They were neither Muslim nor Christian. But, as they tried to understand the Crusades, the only explanation they could find for the Western failure was the nature of Christian religion. In the end, they were so thoroughly convinced of the inferiority of

43

Christianity and the decisive superiority of Islam that they fervently adopted Islam as their religion. [The thinking being that, a true religion must be triumphant over a false religion, no matter what]. With their deep devotion to Islam, they became such furious opponents of Christians as Muslims had never been before. According to Brown (p. 10): "From the acceptance of Islam by Mongols, about 1300 A. D. dates the final and complete estrangement between Christians and Muslims".

Islam and Muslims first marched into India in the first decade of the 8th century. By the end of 12th century, not only the area which is now Pakistan but other areas beyond too had come under the Muslim domination. During this long period, one way or the other, large numbers of the Indian population fell into the Muslim fold. Ultimately, Muslims came to constituted one-fifth of the population.

In Hindu times of Indian History, Ditt's people (from whom most of the Christian converts were later drawn in the 19th and 20th centuries), were treated much as a caste. It was their caste duty to provide hard agricultural labor and perform other services considered low under Hindu rules of piety and social prestige. In return, they received less than subsistence level wages in the form of grain and other handouts at the pleasure of the farmers. They were mostly excluded from social interaction with caste Hindus. They had to live separate and apart in small and modest cluster of houses.

But in Muslim times, things underwent quite a change. For Muslims, the caste system was an unknown phenomenon. In their original Middle Eastern and Central Asian societies there was nothing resembling the caste system. Even more importantly, one of the greatest tenets of Islam happened to be the universal equality and brotherhood of man. Under the circumstances, Muslims of India could not, in good conscience, follow the precepts of caste. But since a large majority of Muslim in India had been gathered from Hindu ranks, traces of the caste system were still in their blood. Consequently, while the institution of caste was not recognized in Indian Islam, watered down precepts of caste did creep in from the back door into the Muslim society.

As is well known, classical Hinduism divided society into four main hierarchical groups or castes, plus a fifth group of "outcastes". The caste division was based purely on occupational prestige and the ensuing socio-economic status. The outcastes, therefore, were those whose occupations were considered so low and so prestige-less as to be devoid of all human dignity, and therefore, unworthy of inclusion in the regular social ranking or caste system. This division was maintained strictly through the fact of birth. This is to say that, one inherited one's caste through the accident of one's birth. The Muslims, on the other hand, practiced a wide open system of social differentiation. One's occupation and wealth were certainly taken into consideration, but the most important criterion for social respectability was the level of orthodoxy that one practiced. And this depended not on one's caste but on one's personal committed-ness to the requirements of Islam. You could be a Syyed, i.e. a descendant of Prophet Mohammed (considered the highest social rank), but if you were a rogue you would be treated as a rogue. All believers were brothers of one another and, as such, possessed equal worth and status. One may be weak, poor, and low-born but that was no reflection on one's person. It is Allah who had made one's life circumstances or *kismet,* and so, did not detract from his inherent personal worth. All believers were equal in the sight of Allah. And a believer, who-ever he may be, is better than a non-believer however rich, powerful, and high-born the non-believer may be.

Thus, under this benign Muslim social philosophy, the lot of Ditt's people (the stock from which most Christian converts were drawn) underwent a change for the better. Their humanity stood largely restored in spite of their badly reduced socio-economic status. The door of Islam was wide open to them, and many chose to enter that door into a spe-cial kind of brotherhood with Muslims. Ibbetson, in his Out-line of Punjab Ethnology (p. 153), points out that, in the 1881 Census, in the area which is now Pakistan, there were 492,000 persons who returned their caste as that of Ditt's but their religion as Islam. Such converts to Islam were called Musallies. [The term Musalli implies being "Muslim like" or "a blurred copy of a Muslim"]. If a Musalli was en-terprising enough, and managed to clime out of his tradi-tionally low existence, he could get admitted into the Mus-lim brotherhood for most practical purposes. As Ibbetson explains, "where a person of low birth was circumcised and became a Mussalman, he was known as a Musalli or a Kotana. The Musalli differed from others of his kind in re-fusing to eat carrion, while the Kotana had some nicer scru-ples still. The Mohammedanism of these people was of a quality that depended on the price of grain. If times were good, and grain plentiful, they converted to Mohammedan-ism, and in Mohammedan villages were admitted to share the drinking water and the smoking pipe of other Moham-medans". Confirming this, the NORTH INDIA NOTES AND QUERIES, a monthly journal of anthropological in-formation, published by Pioneer Press, Allahabad (vol. 11, p. 56), stated that, when times changed for the worse, and the Mussalli was in straits to find a living, he often relapsed into his typically low occupation as that gave him a wider range to derive his subsistence, e.g. he could eat carrion and lizards, while, if times improved, he repeated the Kalama (Muslim creed) and became again a Mussalli. It is easily inferable, that lower classes in Muslim villages were regularly motivated to climb up this social ladder whenever their circumstances permitted.

This open door policy of Islam led some of the lower classes [who were hitherto mainly confined to servile farm labor] to attach themselves as helpers to practitioners of low-skill occupations such as barbers, woodworkers, weavers, leather tanners, cobblers, brick-makers, bricklayers etc. and, in due time, took to these occupations as their regular means of livelihood. But, since most of them still lived in villages, the age old *saip system* remained the most important determinant of their relationship with Muslims, who were also mostly to be found in villages. The hall mark of this system was the abject dependence of these farm workers on the land-owning farmers. Every year a verbal agreement was entered into. The *saipee,* or the worker, would agree to provide all the hard labor required for working the farm. For this, the farmer promised a certain amount of grain plus some handouts to his saipee. Even where the farmer was a good Muslim, and did not wish to demean the humanity of his saipee, the complete economic dependence of the saipee unavoidably made the Muslim farmer arrogate to himself the power of a life sustainer, i.e. *"un-daata* or *"bread-giver"* *(The phrase "un-daata", or bread-giver is, in the strict sense, used for God as He is the ultimate provider).* With such a wide existential gulf between the two, the Islamic sense of human equality was often lost in the shuffle, and the relationship usually slipped into a pattern of power, i.e. a higher humanity on one side, and powerlessness and submission on the other. The relationship between the two, therefore, often assumed caste-like characteristics. The saipees lived in segregated houses. They visited the Muslim houses only when asked to, and usually for work requirements. On special religious and social occasions, they were expected to present their felicitations and receive cooked or raw food items, clothing and, at odd times, even some money. A good saipee would be pride-fully referred to by the farmer and his family, as "our saipee", very much in the sense of a piece of "owned property". And a benevolent farmer would be praise-fully referred to by the saipee as "mie-baap", which literary means 'mother and father' (or benevolent parents).

In summarizing, we may say that, during the period of Muslim ascendancy, the lot of Ditt's people did experience a change for the better. Islam had no tradition of fixing the human worth of a person, or a group, solely because of the accident of their birth. Neither did Islam differentiate between human beings on the basis of the nature of their work. All humans were equal in the sight of Allah; who was man to divide them into worthy and unworthy, or higher and lower. But since most Muslims had Hinduism in their racial and cultural background, they could not altogether rid themselves of the caste-like social differentiation of higher and lower people. But, on the whole their attitude towards lower classes was far more liberal and equalitarian than was ever possible under the Hindu caste system.

As we discuss the shape of Christian-Muslim relations during the early Raj and foreign Missions period, we should recall the Jesuit Missions way back in the reign of King Akbar. We have already noticed that, in 1580, the Great

Mughal invited a Jesuit Mission to his court at Lahore. This was followed by two more Missions from Goa, which continued to operate until 1803. But for all practical purposes, their work was limited to the capital city and the court. This was mainly due to the strong negativity of the Jesuits' attitude toward Islam and Muslims. They derided Islam and Muslims in every which way they could. By and by, the Muslims began to pay back in kind. In angry public debates, the Fathers and Maulanas hurled invectives and abuse on one another. The Fathers so roused the ire of the Muslims that, at one point, they were warned by the King himself, that, if they did not use care and caution, they might forfeit their lives. Instead of reforming their assailing ways, the missionaries gave up on Muslims as a lost cause and, henceforth, confined themselves to serving the European soldiers in the Mughal army and the Western traders in and around the Capital. While the Jesuit episode[1] appears brief, distant, and not very consequential, we can not dismiss it so easily. Oral tradition was very strong in Indian of the day. It is not very likely that subsequent Muslim generations would have forgotten the bitter taste in their mouth left behind by the aggressive attitude of the Jesuits toward Muslims and their religion. It is also highly likely that this early experience might have become part of the future attitudes of Muslims towards all things Christian.

The Portuguese were succeeded by the British. The British East India Company was chartered in 1600. This was the

---

[1] The Roman Catholic efforts, though successful in the enclave of Goa, remained nominal in the mainland. With the coming of the British, Protestant Missions began to dominate the field. Roman Catholic Missions re-emerged early in the 20th century. Presently, Roman Catholics are almost equal in numbers and are a vibrant part of the Christian community in Pakistan.

time when Muslims were still the rulers in India. Though very much reduced in power, a Mughal king still sat on the throne in Delhi. It is true that Company's official interests in India were trade-related. But its personnel had come from a strongly Christian land, and many of them could not easily shed their evangelical interests, especially because many of Company's personnel considered themselves as representatives, or agents, of a committed Christian nation. Company's declared policy was, and continued to remain, non-interference in the religious affairs of India. But many of its personnel could not help but interact with Muslims and others as self-styled ambassadors of Christianity. As such, while taking care not to openly violate Company policy, or to cause ill will among Indians, they did whatever they could to promote the Christian cause. Company's power lasted for more than a century. All through this period, in spite of much pressure from the Mission-minded groups back home in England, company's policy remained that of care and caution; making sure that no religious offence to Indians occurred. Yet quiet and indirect efforts of many of its employees, in behalf of Christianity, continued. Funds were raised and some big and beautiful churches, with steeples higher than any masque minarets in the land were built in major trading centers. These were primarily for use by the British, but were made freely available to others. Some British personnel went to the extent of giving private Christian instruction to enlisted Indians in the British army maintained by the Company.

In 1849, the British took Punjab and completed their control over the entire sub-continent. In the same year, the first organized Christian Mission was inaugurated. Within a relatively short period of time, a number of Mission stations sprang up all over the land, and the missionaries began to engage in highly visible Christian activities and projects. These Mission stations were built on large properties and were comprised of highly conspicuous Western style residences of the missionaries, with rows of servant quarters, and large gardens tended by professional gardeners. They also often included a church, a school building, and well maintained grounds. The missionaries (mostly British and American) began freely to move around the country, and approach Indians in the style and manner of the ruling aristocracy in the land.

At this point, the most serious task before the British was to establish, as quickly as possible, a strong and secure government. For this purpose, they introduced a number of social and political changes. Most of these changes contravened local customs and traditions and, sometimes, seriously violated basic values of the Indian people. The Muslims were the most severely hit by these changes. To begin with, the British Rule had arisen out of the ruins of a Muslim Raj in India. With the displacement of Muslim power, all political influence, economic advantage, and social prestige fled from those classes of Muslims who, during the centuries of Muslim ascendancy had learnt to consider their superiority in the land as an unquestionable reality. From the ruling race, they were now reduced to a national minority. According to Blunt (p. 631 ff), all land grants and estates held by the Muslim aristocracy were confiscated. The traditional Muslim monopoly on military service, a symbol of honor and administrative influence, was also broken and thrown open to Hindus and Sikhs as well. The use of Persian language in the courts was discontinued. Urdu, as the educational and cultural medium in the country was replaced by the use of English language. The enforcement of these changes, eclipsing the Muslim dominance, caused a great deal of soul searching in the rank and file of Muslims of India.

While the people were still struggling to figure out all the consequences of a foreign take over of their country, there appeared in their land a well organized force of Christian Missions clearly protected and boosted by a foreign power, commonly known as the British Raj. There was no other way for the people to interpret all this except that the British had a religious agenda, and that, the Missions were a specialized arm of the British power.[2] Over time, the seed of suspicion over the establishment of Mission and missionaries was driven deep in the psyche of the Indian people. Perhaps the image of Christianity and Christians being a tool of the British Raj and, by extension, of the West, has never left the minds of the natives of the Sub-continent. No where was this suspicion deeper than among Muslims, if for no other reason than that, the missionary campaigns were particularly negative toward Islam. It appears undeniable that missionaries were imbued with the typical Christian prejudice against Islam and Muslims. The study of Mission reports for the years 1849--1855 shows that, adjectives such as "absurd", "impure", "earthly", and "false" were freely used when referring to Islam; and expressions such as "extremely bigoted", "fierce and ignorant", "determined opposers", and "intolerant" were in the daily missionary vocabulary when referring to Muslims. The missionaries were too quick

---

[2] Obviously, the Indian mind perceived the central agenda of the British to be the minimization of Indian resistance to their rule. It appeared obvious to them that the spread of Christianity was a means towards this end. That is to say that, more the co-religionists the British had in the land the wider will become the local sympathy with their Rule.

to run down Islam and Muslims for the smallest excuse they could find. Under such persistent attack, it was natural for Muslims to clam up, and to further insulate themselves against Christian influence of all kinds.

Thus it is that, while Christians and Christianity were met with firm opposition in all quarters of the society, nowhere was this opposition as determined as among Muslims. The Mission Reports of those years indicate the Hindu resistance to be quiet and moderated. But the negative reactions of Muslims were described as open, loud and often severe. The 1856 and 1857 Annual Mission Reports, from Lahore, indicate the prevalence of the feelings of sadness and humiliation because of failure of Christian attempts in wooing all non-Christians but especially Muslims. The first missionary to Punjab had hardly settled down to business before he was urged to remark: "The proportion of those who embrace the religion of Mohammed is much larger than I had supposed . . . There is less prospect of their conversion than of any other class" (Lowrie, p. 131). It was generally believed that a Muslim was born with deliberate and determined resistance to Christianity and Christians. Consequently, Muslims were singled out as the greatest hindrance to the success of Christianity. As such, Hindus were approached with patience and tolerance while Muslims were approached with deep negativity, often with lack of so called "Christian charity". In return, the Muslim reaction toward Christianity was one of rejection, resentment, and even hostility. A Mission Report in 1852 put it this way: "No language seemed too strong to express the hatred felt for the (Christian) doctrines preached . . . Violent and angry opposition was met with almost every day"(p. 19). The Report went on to say that the Muslims were too ready to oppose and contradict anything that the missionaries said or did. The two Mission Reports that followed the 1852 Report asserted that even when Muslims agreed to listen, it was with the purpose to be better able to oppose, and that, all Christian attempts were met with cool and deliberate rejection.

It is clear that Missions and missionaries greatly added to the many and deep frustrations and emotional injuries that had been gnawing at the Indian soul since the British occupation of their homeland. Bitterness and ill will were beginning to spread in every corner of the land. Unfortunately, not a little had been added to the Indian sense of deep fear and alarm by what they saw as a well organized and well funded program of pushing Christianity onto their land. According to Thompson and Garrett (p. 442), "The Government was universally suspected of wishing to convert India to Christianity". Or, as Richter put it (paraphrased), there was a foreboding in the air that the British proposed, by craft or by coercion, to destroy all vestiges of the Indian social system for the eventual Christianization of the country. Let it be said that, this deep suspicion of a surreptitious Christian religious invasion of Indian life and culture became a major source of local aversion to Christianity and Christians.

The smoldering fire of suspicion and fear of religious invasion burst forth into flames when, in 1856, Lord Dalhousie unceremoniously deposed Bahadur Shah, the last Mughal king who, though a puppet of the British, was understood to be the Muslim ruler of India. The incident sent a wave of alarm and panic throughout the length and breadth of the country. Only one feeling prevailed; that India's pride and honor were being ruthlessly wrested from her; that the nation was being treacherously robbed of her power and pride, and being reduced to a humiliating foreign subjugation. While the religious fears were not altogether responsible for the up-rising of 1857 (which is commonly referred to as the Indian Sepoy Mutiny), they certainly aided very much in bringing Indian anger and frustration to an inflammable point; so that, when the spark fell, the rebels and mutineers went to the people with the cry of "*religion in danger*". And they were widely believed. All the rebel proclamations issued from Delhi and Lucknow (the centers of revolt) alluded to the invidious machinations of the British against the creeds of India.

Within a couple of month, the fires of Indian anger and resentment spread to all the major cities in the north-central parts, and even to Punjab proper (the heartland of present Pakistan). The first few victories went to the rebels. They quickly put Bahadur Shah, the last Muslim ruler, back on the throne and proclaimed him king of India. On June 27, 1857, at Meerut, where a number of European families were holed up, General Wheeler surrendered on an ambiguously worded promise of safe conduct to Allahabad. But while the Europeans were boarding boats and barges, the rebel leader Nana's men fell upon them and cut them down to the last man. Women and children were taken alive and confined in Nana's palace at Cawnpore. But soon the British forces, using even greater ruthlessness, began to recapture position after position, and gained the upper hand. When the news arrived that the British were marching on Cawnpore, a deep terror spread every-where. In sheer panic, the palace servants fell upon the two hundred and eleven white women and children held captives in Nana's palace, and mercilessly cut them down. Wild stories of torture, rape, and mutilations committed on the helpless and innocent began to circulate swiftly: "In India, and in England, the news gave a welcome and almost religious sanction to any act of savagery which the British troops might perpetrate" (Thompson and Garrett, p. 454).

No amount of chauvinism can obscure the fact that, the Indian soldiers and, in some cases, even the Indian civilian population, committed heinous acts of barbarity on white Christians. But their guilt appears minor when compared to the heartless brutalities freely committed by the British troops on their Muslim victims. Records show instances of British soldiers sewing up Muslims in pig skins, smearing them with pig fat, and showing them the torch. In Lahore (a Muslim center), some one hundred disarmed rebels took refuge on an island in the river Ravi. Cooper, a British civil official, promised a fair trial if they surrendered. But when they did so, he secured them in a bastion where forty-five of them perished of suffocation, and the remaining were killed the next morning (Thompson and Garratt, p. 454). Townsmen were slaughtered wholesale in the Muslim centers of Lucknow, Cawnpore, and Delhi. An eye-witness has been quoted as saying that, the time of the capture of Lukhnow became a time for indiscriminate massacre; no distinction was made between rebels and non-rebels, mutineer and non-mutineer, civilian or soldier. "The unfortunate who fell into the hands of our troops were made short work of . . . no questions were asked. His skin was black, and did not that suffice? A piece of rope and the branch of a tree, or a rifle bullet through his brain soon terminated the poor devil's existence" (Thompson and Garratt, p. 450).

Mutineers, their active sympathizers, and those suspected of sympathy with them, were mercilessly executed after being subjected to what the TIMES OF LONDON correspondent, in bitter protest, described as "spiritual and mental torture to which we have no right to resort, and which we dare not perpetrate in the face of Europe". After suppressing a mild uprising in Peshawar, on June 10, 1957, "forty prisoners were taken out and blown from guns, and this became the regular punishment for suspected mutiny" (Thompson and Garratt, p. 452).

Hereafter, the feeling of shame, weakness, inferiority, and wounded pride never left the Indians, particularly the Muslims. But the most significant result of the mutiny was the deepening of the religious divide between the bearers of Christianity and bearers of Indian religions, prominent among whom were the Muslims. .

It is well known that far fewer Muslims participated in the Mutiny than Hindus. According to Thompson and Garratt (p. 438) "Of the fifty million Muslims in India scarcely three out of every ten can have rallied to restore their Emperor, Bahadur Shah. The bulk of mutineers were clearly Hindus. Nor is there evidence to prove the acts of barbarism laid to the Muslims. And yet, Muslims were blamed to have been the "real instigators of the Mutiny". It was widely held that a localized dissatisfaction among some soldiers was turned into such a raging fire of hatred and revenge because of the Muslim cries of a Holy War or *jihad*. It was this spirit of Jihad which infected the conflict with religious fanaticism and racial bitterness (Mayhew, p.183). Henceforth, in the eyes of the British, and their sympathizers, Muslims were the proverbial "black sheep" (Kraemer, p.156). It was believed that "the mild Hindu had suffered a temporary aberration" but the Muslims were the "impeccable foe". According to Smith (p. 8) Mutiny left the British convinced that

Muslims were "essentially and religiously disloyal" and rejecting of all things Western and Christian.

With social and political climate remaining what it was, it is easy to imagine Muslim attitudes towards Christianity and Christians during the post-Mutiny period. According to Mission Reports, for sometime Muslims became rather restrained in their opposition. Their open hostility now became indifference, active opposition changed into quiet rejection, and violence turned into scoff and scorn. In other words, Muslims were still resistant and non-conciliatory though not openly acrimonious toward the West and Christianity.

The last years of the 19^h century were perhaps the best years for the British Raj. The Government was relatively secure, and the administrative machinery appeared to be working smoothly. During this period, Muslims were still in a state of withdrawal, quietly licking the wounds to their power and pride. This was also the period when nationalist struggle against the British rule began to be organized on a large scale under the leadership of Indian National Congress. This is also the period when communal struggle of Muslims began to solidify under the leadership of the All India Muslim League. In the political arena, the Christians carried hardly any weight. Therefore, neither the Hindus nor the Muslim cared for their cooperation or support. For one thing, they were too small in numbers. But more than that, their loyalties were suspect.

During all this period of communal strife, Muslims were generally accommodative toward Christians. Also, by this period, the evangelical intensity of Christians, which had been the major source of friction between Muslims and Christians, had died down significantly. Consequently, serious confrontation between Muslims and Christians had become a thing of the past. But the traditional estrangement between the two religious groups was still well and alive. And while Muslims refrained from openly expressing their feelings, the Christian missionaries and local clergy continued their typical approach toward Islam and Muslims. The U. P. Mission's Report for 1903 called them "usual opposers" and "determined hinderers of Christianity and Christians". Without the slightest hesitation, a missionary branded them as "implacable enemies" having "deadly bitterness" toward Christianity and Christians (Stewart, p. 157-58). Similarly, the U. P. Mission Report of 1909 characterized Muslims as bigots of the highest order, and born enemies of Christians. While these instances show missionary attitude towards Muslims, it is hard to imagine that native Christians could have escaped the infectious nature of such attitudes toward their Muslim neighbors.

The communal period was very fast-moving and was marked by an intense struggle between Hindus and Muslims. The Muslims were bent upon dividing the country into two. The Hindus were horrified by such a prospect. In this situation, the insignificant Christian minority had no meaningful role to play. Virtually ignored by both Hindus and Muslims, the Christians hardly played a role in the developments that were under way. Religious politics so dominated the minds of all Indians that all other concerns were pushed way back into the background. In short, we might say that, during the communal period, while the doctrinal disputes between Muslims and Christians remained unchanged, both sides had toned down their rhetoric. Everything in India had boiled down to an unprecedented political drama in the land. The important players in this drama were Hindus and

Muslims. Christians had virtually no role except those of by-standers.

FOUR

Islamism:
Pakistan's Prime Mover

Pakistan claims to be both Islamic and democratic. But the spirit that animates a majority of its people is clearly Islamism rather than anything else.

The original idea of Pakistan is often attributed to the poet-philosopher of Punjab, Sir Mohammed Iqbal. This, however, does not mean that the idea arose in the musings of a philosopher, or in a poet's sudden flash of imagination. In fact, Pakistan was the outcome of the religious dynamics that had been at work in the sub-continent of India for a long time but, more particularly, during the last decades of the 19th and first half of the 20th centuries.

The British power, regarded by most Indians as a Christian power, had been responsible for the undoing of the political and cultural supremacy of Muslims of more than a thousand years. Under the circumstances, while all Indians were distressed, even bitter, over the rise of the British power, Muslims were particularly resentful of all that this new power stood for politically, culturally, religiously, and racially. And as the British hold over India grew stronger and stronger the frustrations of the Muslims grew deeper and deeper.

After the failure of the Indian mutiny of 1857, the country was placed under the direct rule of the British Crown. In due time, thoughtful Indians began to realize that the British Rule was there to stay, at least for the foreseeable future; and that, it was too powerful to be resisted and too useful to be ignored. Nowhere was this realization as widespread as among the Hindus. As a result, they became the first to profit by it. Hindu leaders urged their community to acquire Western education and technical knowledge, and to freely participate in business, trade and, above all, in the huge system of British administrative services. The result was that, before too long, Hindus began to dominate every aspect of Indian national life. This caused a deep dismay among Muslims from one end of the country to the other.

Consequently, when the British decided to introduce representative political institutions, Sir Syed Ahmed Khan, the famous Muslim leader, made it very clear that a system of general electorate "would be attended with evils of greater significance than purely economic considerations". He argued that, "so long as the differences of race[1] and creed formed a major part of the cultural life of India, the welfare of the people must be viewed in reference to those differences". He was of the opinion that, under a system of

---

[1] Most Muslims of the Indian sub-continent are loath to admit that they might have descended from the very large Indian stock of first converts who joined the Islamic ranks during and after the famous Islamic wars and conquests. They rather prefer to claim to be descendants of foreigners from Iran, Afghanistan, Arabia, Turkey, Outer Mongolia, etc. whose ancestors came to India as conquerors.

joint electorate, the larger community would completely override the interests of the smaller community (Symond, p 30). Thus, when in 1885, the Hindus, with the participation of the nationalistic Muslims, founded the Indian National Congress, Sir Syed refused to cooperate. His plea was that the nationalistic aims of the Congress were "exceedingly inexpedient for a country which was inhabited by two different nations". The question according to him was: In case the British should withdraw from India, who would become the ruler, Hindus or Muslims? "Is it possible that under these circumstances two nations, the Mohammedans and Hindus, could sit on the same throne and remain equal in power? Most certainly not! It is necessary that one of them should conquer the other and thrust it down. To hope that both could remain equal is to desire the impossible and the inconceivable"(Symond, p. 31).[2] Perhaps, one can say that, Sir Syed Ahmed Khan's Islamic sensibilities found the concept of religious pluralism, or a secular nationhood, as far too alien, and rejected it out of hand. It appears that, though Muslims had lived together with Hindus for more than a thousand years in the one house of India, shared one basic way of life in a common social milieu, but had never really and truly adopted Indian culture, nor accepted India as their homeland. This strikes one as so very strange, but is quite understandable when one considers the fact that, the foundational concepts of Ummah and Dar-ul-Islam have always prevented Muslims from forming common community with any group of humanity other than Muslims. It is this fact which explains why the self-identity of Indian Muslims, even

---

[2] At the time of partition, Muslims were estimated to be around 19-20% of the population. Though sizable, they were still only a small minority. Thus their claim to be a 'nation within a nation' must have taxed the imagination of many.

63

after a thousand years in India, was never very precisely Indian. They were in India, but not of India since it could not be called Dar-ul-Islam. Thus, there was a strange and unnamable quality about the Indian-ness of Indian Muslims. While it was common place for Hindus to call India as the "motherland", one would hardly ever hear an Indian Muslim use language which would imply his having arisen from the soil of India. For them, it was always Dar-ul-Harab.

In 1906, When the British were considering still wider representation of Indians in the administration of the country, a Muslim deputation, led by Agha Khan, waited upon the Viceroy. The purpose of the deputation was to convince the Viceroy that, in the event of the principle of elections being accepted, Muslims should be granted a separate electorate. A system of joint electorate, the deputation argued, would reduce the Muslims community—larger than many nations of Europe—to a permanent minority. This, they argued, would constitute a gross injustice. The Viceroy accepted the Muslim point of view, and the principle of separate electorate was established in the British Reforms known as the Morley-Minto Reforms of 1909.

Buoyed by this success, the Muslim leadership founded their own communal organization, the All India Muslim League, as a rival to the Indian National Congress. In a matter of a few years, the League had rallied a major part of the Muslim population behind it. The likely prospect of Islam being overwhelmed by another religious group, namely the Hindus, must have proven deeply disturbing to the rank and file of Muslims. Some of the leadership raised the time-tested cry of ISLAM IN DANGER. The appeal of this slogan reached far and wide among the Muslim masses and drove them into the Muslim League camp. Confident of the whole-hearted support of the masses, the League began to challenge the right of the Congress to speak for Muslims of India in any form or shape. By 1929, the Muslim claim to a separate nationhood had become so strong that, in spite of calling it "a serious hindrance to the development of the self-governing principle", the British Government felt obliged to agree to the principle of separate electorate for all religious communities as a guide for all future constitutional developments in India.

The events of the succeeding years brought the Hindu-Muslim conflict to the very brink. In 1930, Sir Mohammed Iqbal, in his presidential address to the Muslim League, advanced a novel idea. According to him, there was no solution to the Hindu-Muslim conflict except by constituting the Muslim majority areas into a separate Muslim state. This proved to be the last nail in the coffin of any kind of pluralism for the Indian sub-continent. Iqbal's idea found the widest acceptance among Muslims. By 1940, Mohammed Ali Jinnah who had, in the meantime, emerged as the "supreme leader" (Quaid-e-Azam) of Muslims, had developed Iqbal's idea into his well known "two-nation" theory. According to this theory, India was a land of two large but disparate communities, each worthy of a separate homeland. In an address to the Muslim League, on March 22, 1940, the Quaid explained his theory in these words: "The Hindus and Muslims belong to two different religious philosophies, social customs, and literatures. They neither intermarry nor interdine, and indeed they belong to two different civilizations which are based on conflicting ideas and conceptions ... To yoke together two such nations under a single state, one a numerical minority, and other as a majority, must lead to growing discontent and final destruction of any fabric that may be so built up for the government of such a state". On the following day, the League formally adopted the "Pakistan Resolution", pledging itself to the unalterable goal of a separate Muslim homeland to be carved out of India. In April, the Quaid reiterated his idea of Muslim nationhood in these words: "We maintain that Muslims and Hindus are two major nations by any definition or test of a nation. We are a nation of hundred millions, and what is more, we are a nation with our own distinctive culture, art and architect, names and nomenclature, sense of values and proportion, legal laws and moral codes, customs and calendar, history and traditions, aptitudes and ambitions; in short, we have our distinctive outlook on life and of life. By all the canons of international law, we are a nation."

In the years that followed, the inevitability of the British withdrawal caused further turmoil. Because of this increasing turmoil in the country, the Hindu-Muslim conflict assumed a new intensity. The Muslim League stepped up its campaign and was able to rally the Muslim masses solidly behind its demand for Pakistan. Towards the end of 1940, the Supreme Leader confidently declared that no power on earth could prevent Pakistan (Symond, p. 60).

In 1945, seeing that the Hindu-Muslim conflict was reaching a boiling point, Lord Wavel, the Viceroy, called a conference of communal leaders—Hindus, Muslims, and Sikhs. His purpose was to bring about the needed understanding and compromise in order to save the multi-ethnic nature of the historic India. But there appeared to be no such will among the leaders. The conference ended in a complete failure. In the meantime, in England, the Labour Party came to power. The first act of the new Government was to order general elections in India. The elections proved an unqualified triumph for the Muslim League. It captured all the Muslim seats in the Central Assembly, and won 466 out of a total of 495 Muslim seats in the Provincial Assemblies. But the elections brought unprecedented Hindu-Muslim clashes in their wake. The Supreme Leader called on Muslims to engage in "direct action". Thousands were killed, looted, and made homeless. Having failed in every peace attempt, and fearing a general upheaval of the worst kind, the British finally accepted the partitioning of the country as the only possible solution to the Hindu-Muslim impasse. On January 3, 1947, a declaration was issued appointing August 15, as the final date for Britain's withdrawal from India. On that day, the control of the country was formally handed over to the successor Governments, and the India of old became two new countries—Hindu India and Muslim Pakistan.

The Christians living in those parts of India, which were to become Pakistan, were indeed a very small community, perhaps around one per cent. They lacked communal organization, and possessed but very small political capital. Nonetheless, whatever little weight they had, they threw it behind the Muslim goal of Pakistan.

At the partition of India, Hindus living in Pakistani areas who felt their position seriously compromised, and their safety threatened, migrated to Indian areas, just as Muslims living in Indian areas who feared for their safety left for Pakistani areas. This un-natural and forced uprooting of people from their ancestral homes was not only heart-wrenching but also proved extremely tragic for the families of at least 500,000 who lost their lives at the hands of communal vengeance-seekers on both sides of the hitherto undefined border. Nearly eight million Muslims fled Indian areas to find refuge in Pakistan. Ten million Hindus fled Pakistani areas to seek new homes in India.

Presumably, Christians were free to migrate from one side to the other. But the very idea of engaging in such uprooting of themselves appeared absolutely senseless. Their roots in the areas where they lived went back to antiquity. These areas had been their ancestral homeland long before there was Islam and Muslims in the sub-continent. Above all, they had known Hindus and Muslims, and had lived with them safely and peaceably for many centuries before their conversion to Christianity, and for nearly a century after their conversion as well. Without a doubt, they were the true sons and daughters of the soil, and the mere fact that the area was to have a new name, and was to be placed under new rulers, did not, at the time, seem to create a strong enough reason for them to pull up their roots and seek replantation in unseen and unknown places, among unseen and unknown people.

Speaking specifically of Pakistan, it is true that there were religious differences between Muslims and Christians, but those differences centered on a few doctrinal issues. Additionally, over the preceding almost a hundred years, there had been sufficient evidence that those differences could be safely lived with under a social order in which basic human rights and equality of citizenship were respected and preserved.

Under the circumstances, the Christian minority in Pakistan could not but be confident that their fundamental rights and liberties would continue to be completely protected, in spite of the fact that the idea of a "Muslim homeland" was not altogether free from some serious Islamist implications.[3]

This great confidence of Christians was grounded in three principal reasons. In the first place, having cast their lot with their Muslim brethren, and being loyal and hard-working citizens, they were pretty sure of their rightful place in the Pakistan-to-be. Secondly, the effective leadership of the Pakistan movement was in the hands of modernist. It was extremely hard to imagine that a state under their leadership could be anything other than a democracy, where all citizens shall be equal in every respect and shall enjoy fundamental human rights and freedoms irrespective of their class, creed, or religious distinctions. The third and perhaps the most important reason was the very person of the "Supreme Leader", the "sole spokesman", and the "sole architect" of Pakistan, lovingly referred to as "Baba-e-Qaum" (Father of the Nation) by every one, from the youngest to the oldest. To this very day, he is revered and idolized as no one else has ever been in the long history of Islam and Muslims in the sub-continent of India.

By all accounts, he was not a religious man. It was commonly known that his Islamic sensibilities were only skin deep. He came from a rich and very cosmopolitan family. He received his early education at a Christian school. His higher education was all in the Christian West. He spent a good deal of his life living in post-Victorian England, and even practiced law there. His mental make-up was clearly that of

---

[3] At the time of partition, the author, as a concerned young man, participated in many discussions among Christian groups. The one conclusion that was reached every time was that, all things considered, Christians should do well in the Pakistan-to-be. The confidence came from the fact that, Islam does recognize Christianity as a true religion though it rejects some parts of it.

a secular rationalist. His public persona inspired every confidence that the Pakistan he was fighting for could not be anything other than a modern democracy. For a major part of his life, he had been a pluralist of the Gandhi-Nehru variety. Nothing in him, or about him, ever raised the slightest doubt about his secular and rationalist credentials. In fact, as far as one could see, his vision of Pakistan appeared to be every bit a secular democracy. The image of Pakistan, projected by him, was that of a "Muslim homeland" only in the sense that it was to be inhabited mostly by Muslims and was to be free of Hindu domination. As to the actual state structure, every word and every action of the "Baba-e-Quam", and his close colleagues, pointed to a truly modern democracy in which the minorities were to be considered a "**sacred trust**".

On at least three known occasions, the Supreme Leader had stated in no uncertain terms that, a Pakistan of the future would be strictly a secular and pluralistic modern state where minority rights and freedoms would be fully preserved. It is commonly known that, in a press conference in Delhi, just a month before Pakistan, a reporter asked the Supreme Leader a blunt question: *Will Pakistan be a secular or a theocratic state?* The maker of Pakistan retorted just as bluntly: *"You are asking me a question which is absurd. I do not know what a theocratic state means"*. It is hard to imagine if there could be a more definitive reply than that? It was no dodge. It was a clarion declaration to the whole world that, Pakistan would not be any thing other than a purely modern democracy without any ifs or buts attached.

Once again, just four days before Pakistan, the Supreme Leader gave his word of honor to all non-Muslim future citizens of Pakistan: "**You are free; you are free to go to your** temples, you are free to go to your mosques or to any other place of worship in this state of Pakistan. You may belong to any religion, caste or creed, that has nothing to do with the fundamental principle that we are all citizens and equal citizens of one state ... Even now there are some states in existence where there are discriminations made and bars imposed against a particular class. Thank God we are not starting in those days. We are starting in the days when there is no discrimination between one caste or creed and another". Continuing, he went on to say: "We are starting with this fundamental principle that we are all citizens and equal citizens of one state. Now, I think we should keep that in front of us as our ideal, and you will find that in course of time, Hindus would cease to be Hindus, and Muslims would cease to Muslims, not in the religious sense, because that is the personal faith of each individual, but in the political sense as citizens of the state" (Bolitho, p. 197).

A few weeks after Pakistan became a reality, he addressed the Constituent Assembly. While highlighting the major challenges facing Pakistan, he made special mention of the need for maintaining law and order "so that the property and religious beliefs of its subjects are fully protected by the State". He then took up the question of minorities. He pointed out that, in the division of the subcontinent between Hindus and Muslims, it was impossible to avoid the issue of minorities. He enjoined the population that, if they worked together "in a spirit that everyone of them, no matter to what community he belonged, no matter what relations he had with them in the past, no matter what his color, caste, or creed, was first, second, and last a citizen of the State with equal rights, privileges,

and obligations", there will be no end to the progress to be made. He ended his speech with this famous declaration for the whole world to hear: **"We are starting from this fundamental principle that we are citizens and equal citizens of one state. You may belong to any religion or caste or creed; that has nothing to do with the business of the state".** Can it ever be doubted that what was being solemnly promised was true democracy with equal rights and privileges for all citizens, irrespective of their race, religion, or social origin?

It is crystal clear that, the Father of Pakistan and his close associates were thoroughly committed to developing Pakistan into an unhampered modern democracy in which absolute equality of citizens, together with guaranteed human rights and civil liberties, was to be taken as a forgone conclusion. How can there be even the slightest doubt that, religion for them was a private and personal matter which played no role in the business of the State. Parse their words whatever way you may, they come out as nothing short of honor-bound commitment to a tolerant, equalitarian, and pluralistic state. These were men of unassailable character and integrity. The truth of their words can in no wise be doubted.

In spite of all this overwhelming evidence, there are two puzzling questions which cry out for answers: Firstly, how is it that Pakistan has turned out to be a state which is, constitutionally speaking, every bit an Islamic Theocracy than a modern democracy? While it is true that Pakistan can lay some claim to procedural democracy, the Islamic Constitution and the Shari'ah Law of the land leave no room for doubt that Pakistan is, in every real sense, a religious state. One may choose to call it what one might, but that does not change the reality on the ground. Secondly, how is it that the people of Pakistan have so easily turned their backs on the "father of the nation" and have chosen to set aside his legacy and have clearly repudiated him? How could they have become so dismissive of him, and how could they have rendered him virtually irrelevant to the shaping of Pakistan while still continuing to call him Baba-e-Qaum (the first father of the nation); and continuing to use his image as the symbol of Pakistan? Knowing what we know about him, it is extremely hard to believe that he could have fathered a Pakistan such as we see today. For this enigma, I offer the following possible explanation:

All through the years of struggle for a separate Muslim homeland, there were two competing ideas that were circulating among the Muslims of India. The idea among the upper leadership, and most of the intelligentsia, was that of a state with the essential features of a full democracy together with some general Islamic adjustments in the personal law area. On the other hand, the idea freely propagating among the Muslims at large, fed by incessant slogans seeped in thoroughly Islamic language, was that of a typical Islamic order with perhaps some minor democratic trimmings. Whether the upper leadership was truly unaware of the Islamist ramifications of the idea of Pakistan, or whether they were too consumed by the idea of "power by any means" is hard to say. The only thing certain is that, they took no effective steps to lay out before the public a precise or clearly defined idea of Pakistan. Consequently, there is little wonder that, the idea of Pakistan that had been steadily firming up in the minds and hearts of most Muslims was that of a state with Islam at its core.

One other thing that suggests itself is that, the upper leadership was so totally dependent on the involvement of the Islamicist masses for the furtherance of their goals that they did not dare disappoint them in any form or shape. In other words, it was virtually impossible to eliminate the centrality of Islam in the idea of a "separated" Muslim Homeland. So they chose to let it lie in order not to lose the crucial support of vast majority of Muslims. There is yet another explanation which has been offered by some Pakistani scholars, such as Ayesha Jalal (Book: The Sole Spokesman). This is that, the upper leadership, most particularly the "Supreme Leader", in their heart of hearts, knew that the demand for Pakistan was too much of a pipe dream and, as such, may never come to pass. Yet they continued to pursue it for the hidden agenda of maximizing Muslim minority's leverage in an independent one-India after British withdrawal. In other words, they knew that it did not really matter what idea of Pakistan was promoted or not promoted since the need to live by that idea might never arise. The partitioning of the land was inconceivable. Thus, while a purely Islamic notion of Pakistan was getting wrought into the temper of a major part of the Muslim masses, the leadership, in spite of all its rhetoric, was not convinced of its coming true. They were content therefore to leave the issue alone *until, and if,* Pakistan ever became a reality.[4]

This wide gulf between the two conceptual images of Pakistan became most apparent as soon as the fundamental

---

[4] The fact that the Muslim League, unlike the Indian National Congress, had not engaged in any pre-planning for the governance of the "proposed" Pakistan, and clearly groped and fumbled for almost a long decade before giving Pakistan even an un-survivable Constitution, tends to lend a high degree of credence to Ayesha Jalal's thesis. [The first constitution took nine years to be born and lasted only a couple of years].

task of constituting the state was put in motion. Tragically for Pakistan, the "father of the nation", perhaps crushed by the remorse over what had been wrought in undoing a multi-religious compact that had taken nearly twelve centuries to build, died within less than a year of the creation of Pakistan. But even during this short period of time he had come to realize the presence of irrepressible Islamic forces which the movement for Pakistan had unleashed and, therefore, had begun to qualify his dream of unfettered democracy by saying that Pakistan would be a "democratic State based on the Islamic principles of justice". (Was he making a distinction between "justice" and "govern-ness is hard to say). Again, just six months after Pakistan, while addressing the Sind Bar Association, he strongly urged his audience to "sacrifice and die in order to make Pakistan a truly great **Islamic State**". Whether these pronouncements were honest reflections of his mind, or whether he had seen an Islamic handwriting on the wall, or whether it was merely an expediency of the moment, is difficult to say. Yet it remains an extreme enigma. The statements simply do not fit the man as he had projected himself to be. He had all his life been a staunch secularist. In his keen legal mind, he must have known all the many and serious ramifications of basing a multi-religious democracy on the principles of justice of any one religion, or of exhorting his audiences, such as the Sind Bar Association, to do their utmost in making Pakistan "a truly great Islamic State". It is also hard to believe that he had reversed himself on his life-long professions of secular democracy. The only plausible explanation for this unseemly "flip flop" appears to be the desperate need of the hour for putting an apparently unlikely[5] new country on its feet, and

---

[5] The original Pakistan was a strangely composed country. It was di-

getting it up and running as a formally constituted state. Perhaps, he had come to the stark realization that, creating one "unified nation" out of a two-part country geographically separated from one another by a thousand miles of foreign territory, the smaller having 56% of the population, with its own language, culture, political aspirations, and a strong sense of a separate peoplehood; and the larger divided into four disparate regional entities each having its own language, culture, economic needs, political traditions, and an historical sense of their own identity was a task which was extremely difficult if not all together impossible. After all, there was only one thread that could keep these divergent parts strung together into any semblance of a nation, and that was the common religion of their people. Therefore, even though contrary to his personal convictions, the Great Leader had no choice but to play the religious card. In many ways, this situation prevails to this day. Religion remains the only significant commonality between the widely differentiated four provincial parts of Pakistan— Punjab, Sindh, Blochistan, and North-West Frontier Province. But just as religion proved an insufficient bond in keeping East Pakistan and West Pakistan together, there is the grave potential of separation between the units of Pakistan as it exists today. In fact, such rumbling is not altogether unheard of. One must remember that, in Pakistan, separatism commands legitimacy since Pakistan itself was born out of separatism. If religion can form the basis of separation between two people so can language and culture. The mother tongues and religious culture in each of the four areas of Pakistan is different and quite distinct. If religious

---

vided into two parts separated by nearly a thousand miles of foreign territory. The Quaid himself called it a "moth-eaten Pakistan".

difference were cause enough for separation between Hindus and Muslims so could language and cultural differences be sufficient cause for separation. Those who live by the sword may die by the sword.

It is well known that Muslim League, as the major political force in Pakistan, was ill-prepared for post-independence tasks of structuring a government. While the Congress party of India had made constitutional, social, and economic plans to be put into operation at attaining independence, Muslim League had no such plans, and was, therefore, hard put to govern a country in which cracks of divisions were already visible to any observer of the situation. Thus, from the very start, Pakistan was gripped with many serious crises. Aside from the major crisis of leadership, there were the crisis of ideological identity, and the crisis of deep divergence between the parts and regions of the country.

Naturally, the first task before the nation was the framing of a constitution. It took two years before the first step in this direction was taken. In March, 1949, an Objectives Resolution[6] was passed in the Constituent Assembly as the ideological guide for the actual framing of the Constitution. Written in the traditional Islamic language, this document was, in effect, a declaration of the Islamic principles of State polity, and showed a large imprint of the Islamist forces in the land. The Islamists, and their followers, uniformly hailed it as the corner stone of a Muslim State. The non-Muslims found it unacceptable and moved a number of amendments. But only one amendment could be carried to a division to be lost badly. Since that point on, the role of Islam in the affairs of the nation has been continuingly present, and the

---

[6] Full text is attached as Appendix B

Islamists have continuingly been successful in holding the State processes as their hostages.

After the passage of the Objectives Resolution in the Constituent Assembly, a Basic Principles Committee was established. The purpose of this Committee was to evolve guidelines for the actual drafting of the Constitution. Once again, the Islamists won the day as no non-Muslim could be appointed to the Committee. While the legislators were struggling to frame a constitution, the Islamists were busy arousing public pressure in favor of a fully Islamic constitution. The modernists attempted to pacify them by setting up a Board of Talimaat-e-Islamia (teachings of Islam) "to advise the various committees on the religious implications of their work" (Gallard, p. 91). The Board was composed of the leading Islamists in the country.

In September, 1950, a draft of the major elements of the Constitution was made public. The Objectives Resolution had given rise to great expectations of a strongly Islamic Constitution. But the draft was not as faithful to the Resolution as had been expected. Obviously, the advice of the Mullahs sitting on the Board of Talimaat-e-Islamia had been ignored. Therefore, the Islamists rejected the Draft out of hand. Soon their leaders were out in the streets inciting the masses against what had been proposed, and denouncing the modernists as betrayers of Islam and Muslims. Seeing that the tempo of Islamist protest was continuing to rise, the Prime Minister announced that the process will be slowed down in order to allow members of the public to make their points of view known. Soon a flood of suggestions began to flow into the office of the Basic Principles Committee. In no time the volume of these suggestions became so great that a special committee had to be set up to review them and to suggest appropriate changes to the proposed Constitution. Most of the public submissions were clearly and strongly in favor of a "more patently Islamic constitution" (Gallard, p. 93).

In the fifth year of Pakistan, 1952, a new draft had been made ready. By April, 1953, while the Constitution was nearing the final stages of adoption, the Government was besieged by a sudden crisis caused by widespread intrigue in the higher circles. In an attempt to head off a very serious crisis, the Governor General dissolved the Ministry, and appointed a new Prime Minister and a new cabinet. However, the crisis continued to paralyze the State processes to such a degree that, in September, 1954, the entire Assembly was dissolved and a new one was put in its place. In order to prevent a repetition of the former impasse, and the resulting state of national paralysis, the modernists found it necessary to yield to the demands of the Islamists.

In the first month of the ninth year of Pakistan (1956), a new draft of the Constitution was prepared and put before the nation. This draft had all the hall marks of a constitution which finally resulted in bestowing on Pakistan a complete Islamist identity. It declared Pakistan to be "an Islamic Republic", and set forth that "no law shall be enacted which is repugnant to the injunctions of Islam as laid out in the Holy Qur'an and Sunnah", and that, "all existing laws were to be brought into conformity with such injunctions". It also laid down that "no person shall be qualified for election as President unless he was a Muslim".

Non-Muslims, as well as progressive Muslims everywhere were dismayed at the religious nature of the Constitution. The non-Muslim members of the Constituent Assembly raised loud cries of foul play, protesting that the Islamic provisions "made the Constitution undemocratic and grossly discriminatory toward non-Muslim citizens". The final debate in the Constituent Assembly took place on February 29, 1956. Again, the non-Muslim members of the Assembly raised a storm of protest. But the Islamists appeared totally oblivious to the existence of non-Muslim minorities. When, at last, the non-Muslim members realized their utter helplessness, they decided to disassociate themselves from the Constitution. They staged a walkout, leaving only the Muslims members to vote the Constitution into adoption. [At that stage, East Pakistan was still a part of Pakistan. With 56% of the total population, East Pakistan had a large Hindu minority that had a noticeable presence in the Constituent Assembly].

It took Pakistan nine long years to put together its first constitution. [It took India only two years to put in place a constitution which happens to be the most detailed of all the constitutions in the world]. But this constitution did not survive for more than two years. The internal strife among the power elite and the political instability which had been rife from the very beginning continued to paralyze the young nation. In the middle of the eleventh year, 1958, the country had reached the brink of a complete collapse. In a desperate attempt to avert the imminent, the President dissolved the Central as well as the Provincial governments, banned all political parties, abrogated the Constitution, and placed the country under martial law. However, the civil structure had deteriorated to such an extent that, within twenty days, a military deputation waited on the President, and obtained his consent to relinquish office and go into exile. General Mohammad Ayub Khan assumed the office of the President.

This was the first of the four military rules that have thus far occurred in Pakistan's relatively short history.

Ayub, the military strong man, was a progressive thinker and, by all appearances, was a secularist at heart. He wanted Pakistan to be as much of a democracy as possible. But the Islamist opposition continued to be formidable. To crush their opposition, he used strong measures. But the more he did this, the more vociferous became the opposition. Day and night they attacked his regime for its lack of legitimacy, and heaped verbal abuse on his person. To silence their incessant drum-beat of venomous criticism of him, in February, 1960, he appointed a Constitutional Commission for a new constitution. The Commission submitted a draft on May 6, 1961. Ayub was not satisfied with the many Islamist features of the draft. He had it reviewed by various committees in the hope of finding support for reducing the predominance of the Islamist provisions of the draft. But, in the end, he had to yield to the Islamist forces. The final version was promulgated on June 8, 1962. The only noticeable victory for Ayub was the changed designatory name of the country from "Islamic Republic of Pakistan" to "Republic of Pakistan". But even this change did not last long. There was too much religious agitation against it. Therefore, before long, the constitutional name of the country was changed back to "Islamic Republic of Pakistan".

While there were some democratic elements in it, the overall Islamic character of the new Constitution remained unchanged: the President had to be a Muslim; the structure of the State had be based on "Islamic principles of social justice"; principles of democracy, freedom, equality, and tolerance were included but only as "enunciated by Islam". Muslims of Pakistan were to be treated as a special group, and were to be enabled, individually and collectively, to order their lives in accordance with the teaching and requirements of Islam. No law was to be repugnant to Islam. An Advisory Council of Islamic Ideology was provided for the guidance of law makers. There was to be an Islamic Research Institute for the purpose of developing ways and means for the promotion of Islam and a truly Islamic society. Once again, the hard Islamists emerged victorious. The progressive Islamists had failed in 1956, and they failed again in 1962 in bringing a respectable level of democracy to Pakistan. Islamism was writ large in the words and intent of the new Constitution.

While Ayub was still having his difficulties with the hard Islamist, another power player was busy spreading his wings. This was Ayub's foreign minister, Zulfikar Ali Bhutto. Bhutto undercut Ayub at every opportunity. In fact, he set up a new party called Pakistan Peoples Party with the express purpose of 'defeating the great dictator [Ayub] with the power of the people'. Consequently, there was continuing unrest in the streets. At long last, unable to control the spreading chaos in the land, Ayub stepped down on March 25, 1969, handing the country to General Yahya Khan as head of a new Martial Law.

Realizing the very explosive situation in the country, Yahya immediately started the process of handing over control to the elected representatives. He announced general elections for October 5, 1970. The elections proved disastrous for Pakistan. Majority of the seats went to a political party based in East Pakistan (which had 56% of the population but was smaller, poorer, and physically separated from West Pakistan by some thousand miles). But the larger West Pakistan was unwilling to cede power to East Pakistan. When the dispute became unmanageable, East Pakistan sought complete independence. West Pakistan took military action to prevent separation. India decided to support East Pakistan. In the end, West Pakistan had no choice but to accept defeat. It appears that the Islamic bond proved insufficient in keeping the two parts bound together. The disgrace of the military (mostly drawn from West Pakistan) made Yahya Khan resign. Bhutto was installed as Head of State.

Bhutto came from a very rich and influential family in the province of Sindh. His father had been knighted by the British and appointed *Dewan* of the Princely State of Junagadh. His early education took place at a Christian school in Bombay. He received his Bachelor's degree at Berkley University in America. He then went to Oxford University and completed his law degree. He was called to the bar at Lincoln's Inn in 1953. Every available indication points to his being a modernist in his thinking and outlook. But, just like others before him, he was challenged by the rigid Islamists in every thing he tried to do. Under the circumstances, his youthful attachment to socialism became his devotion to "Islamic socialism". He tried to transform Pakistani politics by shifting its focus from religious issues to economic issues. But the Islamists were not easily convinced of his being a pukka (confirmed) Muslim, and continued to suspect him of his secularist leanings.

In winning them over, in 1973, he pushed through a new Constitution. Once again, this Constitution went a long way in pandering to the wishes of the Islamists. And in doing so, he became responsible for casting in stone the Islamic character of Pakistan. The bulwark of Islamism was visible right, left, and center in the provisions of the new Constitution. In addition to re-establishing all the Islamic provisions of the preceding Constitutions, the newest constitution set down Islam as the "State Religion", making Pakistan an official theocracy. The fundamental principles of democracy, freedom, equality, tolerance, and social justice continued to remain subject to the injunctions of Islam.

Bhutto was a bright man. But his authoritarian nature often blinded him to reality. His divided loyalties to socialism and Islamism (whatever may have been the depth or nature of his personal Islam), did not serve him well. Soon he was besieged by many problems. In the process of solving them, he actually ended up multiplying them. Before too long, his will power began to crumble, and he began to show himself susceptible to the pressure from the rigid Islamists. In 1972, the insecure Bhutto yielded to Islamist pressure, and dealt the first suppressive blow to the interests of the Christian minority. The rigid Islamists had been raising a baseless outcry that, the Christian schools and colleges were undermining the Islamic goals of Pakistan, distorting Islam's social and cultural values, and corrupting the minds of the Muslim youth. To appease the Islamists, he agreed to their scheme of nationalizing all privately owned and privately managed educational and economic institutions. Under this scheme, his Government appropriated most of the schools and colleges owned and operated by various Christian bodies, and incorporated them into the State education system. In 1974, he yielded to yet another demand of Islamists and proclaimed Ahmadies as a non-Muslim minority. [Ahmadies claim to be a Muslim sect. However, they do not believe in the finality of Prophet Mohammed in the same way as other Muslims do, and advance Mirza Ghulam Ahmad of Qadiann as the last Prophet].

It is quite clear that Bhutto was apprehensive of both the religious establishment and the military establishment. However, in 1977, in the face of mounting opposition and street unrest, he tried to save his regime by appeasing the religious establishment. He made a public promise that Shari'ah Law would be enforced within six months. To prepare the way, he banned drinking, gambling, and nightclubs, and substituted Friday (Muslim prayer day) as the Sabbath holiday instead of Sunday. But even this did not appear to help his power slippage very much. To re-assert his authority, he decided to hold new elections on January 7, 1977. Finding this as an opportunity to oust him, various Islamist forces came together and formed a common front against him, called the Pakistan National Alliance. The PNA mobilized the masses and engaged in widespread public demonstrations and other political actions. From all available indications, Bhutto seemed to be headed for the worst defeat of his life. But when the votes were counted, Bhutto's party came out with 60% of the vote and 75% of the National Assembly seats. The Islamists were stunned. They immediately denounced the elections and charged the Government with stuffing ballot boxes and stealing the elections. When Bhutto refused to pay any heed, they raised the tempo of their protest rallies, demonstrations, strikes, and other public disturbances. Bhutto tried his best to stem the tide, but to no avail. Finding his position weakening day by day, he called upon General Zia-ul-Haq to enforce Martial Law in major centers of unrest. But soon there was a new surprise: On July 5, 1977, General Zia let it be known that the army had taken over the administration of the entire country.

Zia was an educated man though perhaps not as well educated as the leaders that had preceded him. His early education was at a well known school in Simla. His college education was at St. Steven's College, Delhi, again a reputable liberal Christian institution. But, it is difficult to tell whether or not he had acquired any abiding liberal/modern qualities of head or heart. If he had, he never showed them. He projected a public persona of a pious Muslim who faithfully fulfilled all the demands of Islamic orthodoxy. All the same, he was a shrewd man who placed expediency above nicer scruples.

In his first address to the nation, he set forth the Islamic intentions of his regime. He accorded high praise to the Islamic spirit of those who had brought down the previous regime, and asserted: **"It proves that Pakistan, which was created in the name of Islam, will continue to survive only if it sticks to Islam. This is why I consider the introduction of an Islamic system as an essential prerequisite for the country."**

Zia was a m'hajar, i.e. a person who had left his ancestral home in India and had chosen to become a Pakistani citizen at the time of partition. As such, he had no real roots in Pakistan, nor a real home-base or constituency. Under the circumstances, his only source of affinity with Pakistanis was his Islam. Perhaps he borrowed a page from the book of Liaquat Ali Khan, the first Prime Minister of Pakistan. He too was a m'hajar who had no effectual political base in Pakistan and, therefore, had to seek the support of Islamists in order to stay in power. However, irrespective of the real depth of his Islam, it is certain that Zia actively sought to do the will of the Islamists. He declared his mission to be the complete Islamization of Pakistan, i.e. a complete Islamic identity for Pakistan socially, culturally, and politically. Up till now, the Islamization process had been under the care of

Islamic Ideology Council. The role of this Council was merely to advise legislative bodies whether or not any law was "repugnant" to the injunctions of Islam. But Zia's zeal led him to make Islamization a function of the executive branch of the Government. His aim was to place Pakistan under a complete *NIZAM-E-ISLAMIA* (Islamic order of state and society). He promised to see to it that a truly Islamic law was operative in Pakistan. As a first step toward this goal, he announced the establishment of *Shariah Benches* as part of the national justice system. "Any citizen", he announced, "will have the right to present any Law, enforced by the Government, before a Shariah Bench and obtain its verdict as to whether or not a Law is wholly or partially Islamic or un-Islamic". [Shariah is the code of the religious law of Islam].

The Shari'ah Benches are composed of three Muslim judges from the Bar and two Islamic ulema (learned clergy) appointed by the President. These courts are self-regulating and set up their own "proceedings in all respects as they deem fit". Their powers are unprecedented since their decisions **"shall have effect notwithstanding any thing contained in the Constitution".** In other words, they are above the State. A Sharia Court may "either of its own motion or on the petition of a citizen of Pakistan or the Federal Government or Provincial Government examine and decide the question whether or not any Law or provision of Law is repugnant to the injunctions of Islam".

Further, Article 2 of the Constitution which used to read: **"Islam shall be the State Religion of Pakistan"** was very significantly augmented by Zia with the addition: **"and the injunctions of Islam, as laid down in the Holy Qur'an and Sunnah, shall be the supreme Law of the land and source**

of guidance for legislation to be administered through the Laws enacted by the Parliament and the Provincial Assemblies and for policy making by the Government." Simply put, in Pakistan, Islamic requirements shall trump all other principles of law, delivery of justice, and State policies and their execution.

As an aside, two observations need must be made. One, no non-Muslim legal professional, whatever the level of his expertise, is allowed to represent a case or a client before a Sharia Bench. It is forbidden by the Constitution. Two, Sharia Law must be taken as the Law of God. As such, it must be held to be immutable. This is seriously at odds with the conception of law prevalent in the world of today. In modern thought law is considered a living organism which continually evolves in order to retain its relevancy to the changing needs and requirement of society and human culture and behavior.

Basic to Zia's goal of Islamization, among other things, was the promulgation of Hudood Ordinances. These are the typical Islamic Laws which pertain to offences for which there are religiously specified limits of punishments. These laws apply to personal conduct of individuals and are based on Islamic standards of piety. They include drinking and selling of alcohol, punishable with high fine, prison or both; stealing and robbery, punishable with amputation of hands or feet; adultery, i.e. any sexual relation between persons not married to one another, whether voluntary or involuntary, is punishable with stoning to death. Rape is considered adultery unless the raped woman can produce four pious male Muslims who can testify that they saw the act of "forcible" penetration. Short of this bar, the victim must be declared an adulteress and is punishable by stoning. The most oppressive Islamic laws for non-Muslims (and for liberated Muslims), promulgated by dictator Zia-ul-Haq, are the Blasphemy Laws. In total repudiation of such human rights and freedoms as free speech, freedom of conscience, freedom of thought, and freedom of religion, these laws make a blasphemer of any person, even a minor or a mentally deranged person, irrespective of his/her intent and other circumstances, if he/she engages in speech, gesture, act, or any other expression which may be interpreted by a Muslim as offensive to his/her religious sensitivity, or may cast aspersion on Islam or its luminaries. Such a person is liable to be immediately apprehended by any Muslim and brought before a Sharia court for pre-prescribed punishment. [For full text, see Appendix C]

The Zia decade, 1978—1988, must be considered the time when Islamism in Pakistan rose to new heights. In as much as Islamic Law attained primacy, the Islamic identity of Pakistan became a sealed reality. How genuine was Zia's personal Islam? No one can say for sure. But one thing is certain: He has left behind a very unsavory legacy for the non-Muslim minorities of Pakistan, and a lasting scar of intolerant religiosity on the fair face of Pakistan.

Upon his sudden death, Zia was succeeded by Benazir Bhutto. On all accounts, she too must be considered a modernist. Born to privilege, she was educated at Lady Jennings Nursery School and Convent of Jesus and Mary in Karachi. Later she attended Rawalpindi Presentation Convent, and then Jesus and Mary Convent at Murree. She received her Bachelor's at Harvard University and Master's at Oxford University. Obviously, she was a liberated woman with a bright mind and a strong political orientation. Though a pukka (confirmed) Muslim, she did not wear her Islam on her sleeve. Pietistic pretensions were not her forte.

She differed from Zia almost as day differs from night. The hard Islamist of Pakistan, therefore, simply could not stomach her. Neither did the military establishment find her much to their liking. She came to office when ties with Taliban, the purest of the Islamic fundamentalists, were quite prominent in Pakistan. Thus, both the internal and external Islamic forces succeeded in her ouster after only one year in office. She has been quoted as saying: "When I first got elected, they said, "A woman has usurped a man's place! She should be killed, she should be assassinated. She has committed heresy". [Islamic Law does not permit women to be rulers]. She was ousted from office in 1990. In 1993 elections, she got elected again, promising to improve the lot of women and the repeal of the infamous Hudood Ordinances of Zia. But the Islamist and their allies proved too much for her. They hounded her, and constantly kept her off balance in whatever way they could. Most of her energies were spent warding off their attacks on her person, as well as resistance to her policies and programs. Finally, in 1996, her Government was dismissed under exaggerated charges of corruption by the President who had Islamist leanings. And thus, another modernist was done in by the Islamists.

In the ensuing race for leadership, Benazir Bhutto was succeeded by Nawaz Sharif. It is difficult to identify Nawaz's ideological make-up. But one can say with a degree of confidence that, he was an Islamist as and when it served his purposes. He was the leader of a splinter group of the Pakistan Muslim League, the mother of all political organizations in Pakistan. Perhaps wealth and influence were his greatest assets.

During his military rule, Zia had appointed Nawaz as the Finance Minister of Punjab. Later, he rose to be the Chief Minister of Punjab. When in 1990, Benazir was removed from Office, Nawaz came to power as the Prime Minister of Pakistan. In 1993, the President dismissed his Government under charges of corruption and cronyism. In the 1996 elections, Nawaz won a convincing majority and became the Prime Minister once again. He was the first ruler with deep roots in the Punjab Province, the largest ethnic population block, the most developed area in all of Pakistan, and where Islamism has very deep roots. He was quite cozy with the Islamist and frequently promoted their agenda. The Islamization of the nation, particularly in the cultural, social, and legal areas continued to advance under his wings.

But Nawaz was given to overplaying his hand. In addition to his well known feud with the President, he also entered into an open conflict with the Chief Justice. At one time, his goon squad swarmed the Supreme Court threatening to kill the Chief Justice. Similarly, he had rocky relations with the Military establishment. In course of time, the friction between him and the General Staff of the army became serious. In 1999, when General Parvez Musharraf, was out of the country, Nawaz tried to replace him. Musharraf got wind of the matter and immediately chartered a plane to get back to Pakistan. When Nawaz ordered the airport administration to prevent the plane from landing, Musharraf ordered the army to cease the airport, and the plane landed safely just in the nick of time. Musharraf declared Martial Law. Nawaz was charged and convicted of tax evasion, corruption, hijacking a plane, and terrorism. His life was spared but he was debarred from holding office for 21 years and was fined twenty million rupees. Additionally, he was to remain behind bars for 14 years. But, in the end, Musharraf agreed to grant him exile.

Musharraf started his rule as both the head of the military and the "Chief Executive" of the country, a transitional title which he created for himself. But within a couple of years, he worked himself into the Presidentship of the country. Upon taking control, he issued a proclamation placing the Constitution in abeyance, putting the whole of Pakistan under the control of the Armed Forces of Pakistan, and installing himself as the Chief Executive of the Islamic Republic of Pakistan. In pursuance of this proclamation, he issued his first order regarding a Provisional Constitution. The important features of this order were: (1) That, while the constitution was held in abeyance, its selective application will remain in tact; (2) All the courts (including the Shariat Courts) "shall continue to function and to exercise their respective powers and jurisdiction"; (3) The Fundamental Rights conferred by Chapter 1 of Part 11 of the Constitution "shall continue to be in force"; (4) "Notwithstanding the abeyance of the provisions of the Constitution, but subject to the Orders of the Chief Executive, all Laws other than the Constitution shall continue in force until altered, amended or repealed by the Chief Executive or any authority designated by him". Within two years of assuming control as the Chief Executive, Musharraf worked himself into the Presidentship of the country.

Musharraf was born to a middle class family of Delhi. At Partition, the family crossed over to Pakistan and took up residence in Karachi. Musharraf was only four then. His next few years were spent in Turkey where his father was posted as staff member at the Embassy of Pakistan. Back in Karachi, he attended St. Patrick's High School. Later, the family moved to Gujranwala in Punjab. For his college education, he went to Lahore to attend Forman Christian College. Immediately after coming to power, he declared his goals to be the stabilization of the country, rooting out corruption and sectarian violence, rebuilding the economy, and bringing "true democracy" to Pakistan. In nine years of his rule, while he succeeded in some of his objectives, his success in rooting out corruption, violence, in-fighting, and in bringing true democracy to Pakistan, remained very limited.

He was the first ruler who advanced an ideology of "enlightened moderation" not only for Pakistan but for the entire Muslim world. In an article in The Washington Post, dated May 31, 2004, he acknowledged that Islam was glorious only when it followed equalitarian, humanitarian, secular and democratic values and shunned intolerance and violent extremism. "Today's Muslim world is distant from all these values. We have been left far behind in social, moral, and economic development. We have remained in our own shell and refused to learn or acquire from others. The result of all this is that Muslims have reached the depth of despair and despondency". The only way forward for the Muslim world, he declared, is self-development through modern education, renunciation of violence, and commitment to social justice. "If this is our direction, it cannot be achieved through confrontation. We must adopt a path of moderation and a conciliatory approach in order to fight the common belief that Islam is a religion of militancy, in conflict with modernization, democracy, and secularism". This, he held, must be done with the realization that fairness cuts both ways. We cannot demand fairness from others without first being fair to them.

Upon close examination, one is likely to conclude that, while Musharraf desired expansion of democracy in Pakistan, he also sought a sizable role for Islam in the affairs of the State. Perhaps, he realized that, Islamism runs deep in the veins of Pakistan, and it will take a long time of slow transfusion of progressive modernism before the nation, as a whole, will become receptive to the ways and demands of true democracy. Seemingly, he believed that, religion and democracy can go hand-in-hand. As we have noted above, he publicly asserted that Islam is not necessarily incompatible with democracy. At the same time he admitted that, the kind of Islamism which is self-adulating, is above and beyond the pale of self-criticism and objective self-evaluation, and has a fortress mentality is necessarily unsuited to the open, tolerant, and free ways of democracy. His exhortation to his fellow Muslims appeared to be to abandon their isolationist ideas simply because in the world neighborhood the House of Islam does not, or can not, exist by itself. There are other houses and other residents in this neighborhood. And, if most residents of this neighborhood have chosen to live the secular and democratic way of life, then, in the interest of neighborhood harmony, the House of Islam owes it to itself to give such democracy a long, hard, and open-minded look. After all, one has hardly a real choice but to live peaceably with one's neighbors. This trait, he asserted, is nothing new to Islam. Islam's glory days were those when it embraced liberal and secular values, and approached other religions and civilizations as realities to be accepted and adjusted to with tolerance and complete grace.

All in all, Musharraf had been, comparatively speaking, a progressive ruler. During his time in office, Musharraf tried to soften the impact of laws that were detrimental to the interests of vulnerable groups, including women, children, and religious minorities. He succeeded in removing separate electorate for religious minorities which was a blatant exclusion of minorities from the national body politics. He also succeeded in lessening the affect of Shari'ah Law of Zinah (adultery) which subsumes rape. The irrational confusion of illicit sex with rape caused all kinds of horrifying injustices to the women of Pakistan, particularly the women of minority communities whose rape was regularly twisted into their own entrapment of men for illicit sex.

Towards the end of 2007, Musharraf's regime began to come under constant attack by former leaders who had been driven into exile after his assumption of office as the President of Pakistan. Under tacit pressure from USA, former Prime Ministers Benazir Bhutto and Nawaz Sharif were allowed to return to Pakistan and resume political activity and participate in elections. Thus, when by all apparent signs, Bhutto was poised to win the next election and become the Prime Minister, her opponents were horrified at this prospect. So on December 27, she was assassinated. Once again, violence had the upper hand in Pakistan. Consequently, elections were put over to February 18. The murdered Bhutto's party (Pakistan People Party) won the highest number of seats, with Nawaz Sharif's Muslim League (Nawaz faction) coming second. The Muslim League (Qaid-e-Azam faction), the backers of Musharraf were virtually wiped out. A coalition between PPP and Muslim League (N) formed the government with Yousaf Raza Gillani as the prime minister.

In the early months of its power, the new regime, particularly the Nawaz faction, could think of nothing else but the removal of Musharraf' from office. When he resisted, they prepared impeachment papers, and fixed a date for starting the proceedings. Under mounting pressure, Musharraf finally resigned on August 18, 2008. On September 6, election for a new president was held. Asif Ali Zardari was elected the new President of Pakistan. Up to now, Zardari's claim to greatness has been that he is the surviving husband of the murdered Benazir Bhutto. Therefore, it is hard to tell what kind of leader he will prove to be. How deep will be his devotion to promoting the Islamic nature of Pakistan? Or, put in another way, how deep will his democratic sensibilities be, and to what extent will he be prepared to defend and promote the fundamental rights and freedoms of small religious minorities in Pakistan?

We close this chapter with the following observations: Regimes will come and go. Some will be more progressive than others. Each will handle the "given" role of Islam according to the depth of their commitment to Islamism. Or, otherwise, according to how deep are the Islamist forces in the land that a regime must contend with? Given the insufficient spread of modern education in the land, and given the deep roots of religious fundamentalism among all but a small upper class, the essential modern values will take a long time to take roots in the land. To become modern, a nation must strike a viable working balance between religious/static values and secular/dynamic values. Thus far, such a development has eluded Pakistan. Islam remains the one foundational reality which appears to reside deep in the very soul of Pakistan, both as a state and a society. Deviating from the path of Islamism, which Pakistan has clearly followed ever since its emergence, and which has bestowed upon it a firm Islamic image, is not something from which it can easily extricate itself. Religious "purism" was, is, and continues to be the only ground for Pakistan's existence. There is no determinable basis on which it may be said that Pakistan will put aside its Islamism and still stand justified as a "partitioned" homeland of Indian Muslims. Thus, given the supremacy of Islam, and of the Islamic ideology as enshrined in the Constitution, Christians and other religious minorities in Pakistan, will always be open to inequality of national status as well as discrimination in regard to their basic democratic rights and freedoms. No doubt, the Islamic Constitution of Pakistan guarantees equality before the law, and promises basic rights and freedoms. But the Constitution is only a piece of paper; a declaration of a set of high sounding principles. What really makes a difference is a strong set of clear and equitable statutory laws and, even more so, a complete willingness to live by those laws.

FIVE

The Christian Situation in Pakistan: An Overview

Briefly put, the situation of the Christian community in Pakistan may be characterized by five main realities: 1) insignificant numbers; 2) lack of social prestige; 3) low economic ability; 4) marked political marginality; 5) a nagging sense of powerlessness and vulnerability, or being weighed down by a sense of excluded-ness.

During the first decade of Pakistan, the life situation of minorities was very much the same as it had been in pre-Pakistan (British) times. This was the time when Pakistan had no constitution, nor its own law. It was still governed under Britain's Government of India Act 1935. Under that Act, equality of citizenship was guaranteed to all, irrespective of their race, religion, or social origin. During the first decade of Pakistan, therefore, though the traditional differentiations had continued to exist, they were not allowed to affect the weaker religious groups in regard to their safety, security, and a place in society.

The Christian Minority in Pakistan

As time moved forward, there were high hopes that, life for minorities will continue to be as safe and secure, and as free from encumbrances as it had previously been. Somehow, minorities were banking on the development of a full democracy in which human rights for all citizens would be fully preserved and promoted. It was hard for Christians, the most visible minority, even to imagine that Pakistan could turn out to be anything other than a true democracy. After all, this is what had been so loudly and so proudly proclaimed by the Quaid-e-Azam, the "creator of the nation" and the "sole spokesman" for Pakistan. By his given word of honor, Pakistan was to be a state in which there was to be absolute equality of all citizens, and in which protection of human rights and freedoms of weaker groups in society was to be taken as a foregone conclusion.

But the high hopes of minorities began to fade when Islamism began to surface as the raison d'etre for the creation as well as the existence of Pakistan. Even the solemn avowers of democracy soon began to veer off into the pursuit of Islamic goals. And the promise of Pakistan, as a *"Muslim homeland"*, which many middle and lower level leaders had been freely holding out to the Muslim masses, began to demand its fulfillment. It appears that, this promise of a "Muslim homeland" had, wittingly or unwittingly, pre-ordained an extensive role for Islam in the structuring and functioning of the new State. In other words, it had become quite impossible for Muslims of Pakistan to think of Pakistan without presupposing a very large degree of Islamism in its make-up. There is hardly any wonder then that, over the entire history of Pakistan, Islamism has been the most significant reality in all matters of State and society. It is not being suggested here that liberal or democratic thinking has been totally absent from Pakistani national affairs. But no one can deny the fact that such thinking has always been seriously overshadowed by a noisy and persistent Islamism. The Objectives Resolution (Appendix B), with its deep Islamic import, has remained the foundation on which the Pakistani State has continued to be grounded.

Thus, it is hardly surprising that, all through its life of six decades, while it has maintained a semblance of democracy (through what is known as "procedural democracy'), the dominant reality in Pakistan has been its heavily Islamic character, both as a state and as a society. In fact, in 1973, through its third constitution, Pakistan officially turned itself into a full-fledged Islamic theocracy. Laws, law making, principles of justice, and the administration of law and justice have all been placed squarely under the dictates of Islam. Once again, the attention of the reader is drawn to Article 2 of the Constitution: "Islam shall be the State Religion of Pakistan, and the injunctions of Islam as laid down in the Holy Qur'an and Sunnah shall be the supreme Law and the source of guidance for legislation to be administered through the Laws enacted by the Parliament and Provincial Assemblies, and for policy making by the Government".

Obviously, in Pakistan's Islamic state structure, religious minorities have been rendered as second class citizens, and perhaps even worse. Their unequal national status seriously affects their ability to obtain equal, or timely, protection of the Law, or to approach and receive full justice from the justice system which, in any event, is too costly to afford and too convoluted to navigate. Thus, a non-Muslim, being a "lesser citizen" can never be confident of receiving the degree of protection, or the level of justice which he/she may be otherwise entitled to.

THE CHRISTIAN MINORITY IN PAKISTAN

In the early years, things had not been too worrisome for Pakistani Christians. Of course, there had been some scattered cases of harassment of but nothing too alarming. However, things took a turn for the worst following the events of 9/11/2001. Goaded by the presumed Islamic success of 9/11, and the Jihadic pronouncements of Osama Bin Laden, Muslim extremists in Pakistan went into an avenging mode against the Christians of Pakistan, attacking even worshipping congregations in the Churches. Identifying the Christians of Pakistan with the Christians of the West, they committed acts of Islamic punishment on them, causing death and destruction.

In the pre-9/11 period, the instances of maltreatment of Christians in Pakistan were few and far between, arising mostly from personal disputes which often assumed the coloring of religious conflict. But after the events of 9/11, such instances began to assume the shape of willful aggression by fanatical Muslims. And Christian vulnerability to this aggression began to be more visible than it had ever been before. The crisis seems to have tapered off. However, random Muslim aggression against Christians still persists. We must note that, the Government, the legal and judicial system, and most members of the Muslim community are well disposed towards Christians, and are mindful of their national rights and liberties. It is only those who are under the sway of less enlightened Muslim clergy who somehow consider themselves as doing the will of their religion by committing harm on weak and often unsuspecting and isolated Christians. Therefore, the reader is warned not to come away with the impression of systematic Muslim aggression against Christians. It is certainly true that sporadically Christians do suffer at the hands of Muslims. But it must be emphasized repeatedly that such aggression is purely random or incidental. This, however, does not mean that acts of aggression perpetrated on Christians, especially when they occur as a result of a lack of sufficient Governmental protection, should go unnoticed. Such cases have been abundantly documental by highly reliable third party sources and are commonly known to the world.

By way of a general statement, let it be said that, the Constitution of Pakistan provides for freedom of religion, and sets forth that, adequate provisions shall be made for religious minorities to profess and practice their religions. But, in actuality, there are few such provisions and their enforcement often falls short of the required degree of promptness and sufficiency. Constitutionally, the Country is an Islamic Republic, and the Constitution requires that the laws be consistent with the requirements of Islam. This naturally places a number of susceptibilities on the small and weak Christian minority. For example, in Islamic tradition, actions or speech of a non-Muslim, occurring anywhere in the world, binds every "good Muslim" everywhere to avenge it. Thus, there have been cases when something derogatory to Islam or Muslims has been said or done in a far off country and Christians of Pakistan have been made to pay the price..

Religious freedom does exist in the Constitution but it has been made subject to Law, public order and morality. In other words, it has been subordinated to Islamic sensitivities, Islamic tradition, and Islamic moral precepts. Accordingly, actions or speech deemed derogatory to Islam or its Prophet are not protected. Further, no law can be passed which is not consistent with the requirements of Islam. In other words, Islam remains the core element in the country's national ideology. All senior officials, from President down, are required to swear an oath to preserve the country's Islamic ideology. Freedom of speech is theoretically provided for, but has been constitutionally made subject to restrictions *"in the interest of the glory of Islam"*. Actions and speech considered disrespectful toward Islam (and by implication toward Muslims) are prosecutable; and any act, word, or gesture deemed disrespectful towards the Holy Prophet Mohammed carries death sentence.

By far, the most potent sources of fear and trepidation for Christians are the loosely defined Blasphemy Law and the Hudood Ordinances. Muslim rivals of Christians, and Muslim vendetta seekers, have freely used Blasphemy Laws to threaten, abuse, exploit, or hurt members of Christian minority. Once a blasphemy charge, even a fictitious one, is brought against a Christian, he/she becomes a target of the Muslim extremists, even onto death. When in 2000, under international pressure, President Musharraf proposed to amend even the procedural aspects of these laws, there was a sever reaction from Islamists. They issued a blunt warning that, if any part of the law was changed, they would take matters into their own hands and would kill off blasphemers before they could even be brought before the courts.

Obviously, life under these conditions is quite constricted for Christians of Pakistan and, indeed for all minorities. The Government, by and large, fails to fully protect the rights of minorities. This is due both to public policy and to the Government's inability or unwillingness to take effective and often unpopular actions against societal forces hostile to those who happen to follow a faith other than Islam. One specific failing of Government is to take no action for the abolition of the draconian Hudood Ordinances and the

Blasphemy Law which grossly discriminate against non-Muslim minorities. The Government does not encourage societal violence against religious minorities, but neither does it take decisive actions against it when it does occur. This persistent lack of decisive response by the Government obviously creates an atmosphere of impunity for acts of violence and intimidation committed against the Christian minority, small groups of which are scattered through out the far flung parts of Pakistan.

It goes without saying that every Christian in Pakistan lives under a constant fear that, somehow, somewhere, under some circumstance or another, he/she is going to be hauled in by the drag-net of the much dreaded Blaspheme Law, or the Hudood Ordinances, no matter how super careful he/she may be. It is well established that, religious minorities are afforded fewer legal protections than Muslim citizens. The judicial system is too complicated and almost always less receptive or sympathetic towards Christians. The Hudood Ordinances, which include sexual offences, are applied to Muslims and non-Muslims alike. While minorities constitute no more than three percent of the population (census 1980), twenty-five percent of the cases filed under the blasphemy laws pertain to religious minorities, mostly Christians. According to the center for Legal Aid Assistance and Settlement (CLAAS), non-Muslims apprehended under Blasphemy Law are put in jail right away, without any possibility of bail for fear that Muslim zealots might take matters into their own hands and might murder them before the Courts have had a chance to settle the matter. While in custody/jail, minority persons, especially Christian, are often handled with a very heavy hand.

THE CHRISTIAN MINORITY IN PAKISTAN

The Ministry of Religious Affairs, which is entrusted with safeguarding religious freedom of minorities, has on its masthead a Qur'anic verse which says: **"Islam is the only religion acceptable to God"**. The far reaching implications of this are not too hard to see. Obviously such official acts put a seal of rejection on religions other than Islam. Under the circumstances, human rights present a very serious problem in Pakistan. In fact, human rights monitors believe that a narrow interpretation of Sharia Law has clearly had a harmful affect on minority rights as it reinforces popular attitudes and perceptions, and contributes to an atmosphere in which discriminatory treatment of non-Muslims is accepted quite readily. Governmental authorities afford religious minorities fewer legal protections than are afforded Muslims. Members of religious minorities are subject to violence and harassment, and police at times refuse to prevent such occurrences or to charge persons who commit them.

It is not the aim here to recite a litany of all the cases of Muslim high-handedness or aggression to which Christian individuals or groups have been, and continue, to be subjected. These are universally known and continue to be amply documented by such highly objective sources as the yearly reports of the US Department of State (International Religious Freedom); US Country Reports on Human Rights Practices; Amnesty International Reports; The Voice of the Martyrs; and various other such highly objective and highly reliable sources[1]. It is well known that, human rights in general, and religious freedom in particular, have been, and continue to be undermined in various and sundry ways. Over the years churches have been attacked, worshipping Christians have been killed, and religious books and arti-

---

[1] These sources have been relied on, both for content and language.

facts have been torched. Christian women have been harassed and abused in the work place, in the streets, and even
in the church compounds of isolated small places. Christian
girls, as young as twelve, have been carried off and raped.
Others are lured or forced into fake marriages only to be
abandoned after a short fling. There have been numerous
cases where a Muslim has brought a false blasphemy charge
against a Christian co-worker, neighbor, competitor, or con-
tender either to extract a selfish gain or to feed a vendetta. A
general climate of discrimination prevails in all areas of life
including personal, economic, and social. Regimes have
come and gone, but this atmosphere of Christian vulnerability has continued unabated. Christian honor, Christian liberty, and Christian security appear to be permanently at risk.
Just to provide an idea of the vulnerability of Pakistani
Christians we cite three most recent cases of lawless acts
committed against them: In the District of Sahiwal there is a
small village of land-owning Christians—Chuck 190-91.
The general area is known for its Islamic fundamentalism.
In 2008, a Muslim gang attacked the house of Maqbool Masih (a Christian), looted the contents, and holding him at
gunpoint, carried away his young daughter, Noshi.
Maqbool Masih's efforts at finding the whereabouts of his
daughter have been utterly frustrated. Lately, however, a
Christian lawyer, Javed Sohotra has agreed to approach the
Session Court for the production of Noshi and the resolution of the case. Similarly, on October 9, 2008, a large crowd
of Muslims attacked a Church, throwing rocks, firing guns,
and shouting: "death to Gulsher Masih and Sandul (his
daughter). They accused Sandul of tearing pages from the
Qur'an in violation of the Blasphemy Law. The incident was
broadcast from mosques in the area, inciting Muslims to

avenge the disgrace committed against the Holy Qur'an. The crowd was set to burn down the house, with Sandul and her father in it when finally the police came and arrested Sandul and her father. They are still in jail and no one knows what will be their fate. Again, in February of 2009, two Christian nursing students at Fatima Memorial College, in the city of Lahore, had hung a picture of Jesus in their room. This displeased the Muslim students. They demanded that the picture be taken down. When the Christian girls refused, the Muslim girls tore up the picture and threatened to take to the streets demanding that the Christian girls be publicly whipped. When the hostel warden, herself a Christian, tried to intervene, the Muslim girls turned against her. The three Christians managed to escape. They have now been expelled from the College under a fake charge that they tore a page from the Holy Qur'an and threw it in the garbage. [This act is a chargeable offence under the Blasphemy Law, the most pernicious law that acts as a choke-hold on Christians]. As recently as August 2, 2009, The Observer (London) reported that six (later reports said seven) Christians were burned alive in Pakistan when hundreds of Muslims attacked, looted, and torched Christian homes, sparked by false rumors that pages from the Qur'an had been desecrated by Christians. The six/seven killed included four women and a child. Around fifty Christian homes were burned to the ground. Tensions had been running high due to Muslim allegations that Christians had defiled pages from the Qur'an despite authorities' insistence that the rumors had no basis in fact.

Nearly three weeks after this glaring case of Government's inability, or unwillingness, or both, to provide effective protection to law-abiding Christians, one Muslim voice rose in protest. Naveen Naqvi said in the Dawn of August 18th that there had been a series of reports of Christian persecution. She bemoaned the fact that the atrocities at Gojra had been committed by the "banned" Sipah-e-Sahaba and Lashkar-e-Jhangvi. She further expressed her disgust since these fundamentalist organizations are legally banned, and asked the question: What good is the ban if there is no will or ability to enforce the ban? Once again, we are obliged to affirm our hypothesis that, as long as Islamism possesses the "street power" in Pakistan, the potential of violence against Christians, government or no government, law or no law, will remain.

Internally, the Christian community is very small, weak, and without resources. Possibly about 1.7 % of the population, they are scattered all through the far flung parts of the country. An estimated one-fifth or more live on modest income derived from the prestige-less profession of street cleaning. The rest are in daily wage work, or in low paying jobs. There are precious few in business and fewer still in professional fields or civil services. The former requires capital which they don't possess; and the latter requires "connections", or a prominent Muslim patron or promoter. Both are usually beyond the reach of Christians. An unspoken attitude exists in Muslim minds that, since Pakistan was created exclusively by Muslims and for Muslims, they have a prior right to every economic and social opportunity in the land. In fact, many of the less informed Muslims believe that only Muslims can be the rightful or true citizens of Pakistan. All non-Muslims, therefore, are merely "accidental" or second class citizens.

Approached differently, perhaps one can say that, the Christian problem in Pakistan is a composite of several factors. Some of these factors are external and some are internal. The most significant of the external factor is the low social image that attaches to the pre-conversion life of a part of the community. Put differently, a large part of Christians are looked upon as having come out of a prestige-less section of society—chronically poor, excluded, and worthy only of subservience to others. Under the circumstances, they are hardly ever taken seriously. To make things worse, they are not well integrated into society, neither socially nor culturally. It is true that only a very small portion of them are now left in their pre-Christian low occupational life. But Muslims still continue to see all Christians as chips of this old degraded block; and do not hesitate to through this in their face including even those Christians who have arisen above many a Muslim. Strange though it may seem, even after almost hundred and fifty years, Christians continue to be seen as intrinsically substance-less entity. Perhaps one may go so far as to suggest that, Christianity and Christians are largely seen as a West-created, West-maintained, and West-oriented factor in Pakistan with very little "local" significance.

Another part of the image of Christians derives from the historical controversy between Islam and Christianity. The arrogance of the Christians to refuse to recognize the bona fide of the second largest religion in the world remains a serious source of Muslim estrangement. While Islam and Muslims do recognize and acknowledge, to a very large extent, the truth of Christianity, Christians remain adamant in their refusal to accord due recognition to Islam. This deep and perpetual Christian negativity causes Muslims to be resistant to Christians.

Yet another part of the image problem resides in the perceived foreign-ness of Christianity. It was and, very largely, continues to be linked to its foreign origins. In fact, the essence of its entire nature is foreign to the religious culture of Pakistan. No doubt Christianity first arose in the East, but when it was brought to the Indian sub-continent, it had been so thoroughly Westernized that it could not be recognized as an Eastern religion. In 1912, Rev. D.T. Bradley (later bishop of Allahabad) collected Christian opinions about Christianity in the sub-continent. One of the most revealing comments came from Henry Foreman, himself a prominent missionary: "The Church in India is so foreign in its organization, its terminology, the dress and appearance of its members, that it cannot be called Indian by the people of India" (THE INDIAN CHURCH, unpublished collection of opinions, Allahabad, 1912, p. 4). In 1914, a similar comment came from a great Indian nationalist, Lala Lajpat Rai, a leading mind in the sub-continent. While referring to the foreignness of Christianity, he described Indian Christians as "those who are neither with us nor of us". In 1919, writing on "The Indian Christian Community and it Future", (THE INDIAN INTERPRETER, October, p. 140), Lamuel L. Joshi, an Indian Christian, said this: "The Christian religion in India, as we see it lived today before our eyes, bears on every hand the marks of the foreigner. The Indian Christian tends to become a foreigner in his own land, cut off from his own people. He not only deserts the religion of his fathers and forefathers of countless generations but he also abandons the customs, traditions, mode of life, eating and drinking and even dress which distinguishes Indians and makes them a distinct type of human civilization". To this may also be added the words of an early missionary: "Christianity appears in India as a foreign religion; buildings are foreign in design, Christian literature is foreign; in Church government the control continues to be in the hands of White men ....Christianity is an exotic ...".

These and many other instances, which we have alluded to, clearly indicate that, Christianity has never been perceived in the Indo-Pak sub-continent as compatible with local social and cultural forms. In fact, it has been looked upon as so very un-local, perhaps even anti-local, that most local people have been unable to look upon it, or its followers, as capable of belonging in the local milieu.

In one very significant sense, Christianity in Pakistan has the image of a failed religion. As has been observed earlier on, the Christian work was begun in the cities with the express purpose of concentrating all efforts on the educated classes and people of good social standing. It was believed that the success of the enterprise depended on first winning "the leading minds" in society (Clark, p. 3). That, if people of better social classes were first won over, the task of winning over the lower classes would present hardly any problem (Pickett, p. 56). But decades went by without any success with the better classes. In thirty-one years, Gordon, one of the pioneers, could count only fifty inquiries from upper classes (less than two per year). In spite of no effort being spared to woo them, all but three of the fifty soon fell away. The same source later recalled: "Concentration on the upper classes failed to produce the hoped for results". Still more telling are these words of A.P. Mission Report of 1856 (p. 26): Referring to work among upper classes, the report said: "It is sad and humiliating to record year after year that our labor has been, so far as we can see, almost in vain". Ten years later, the prospect was still described as "so very dark and discouraging" (Gordon, p. 212). In 1871, one of the oldest Missions referred to its negligible success in these words: "There is something very startling in these figures. It would be vain to deny that they afford us cause, not only for profound regret, but for unfeigned self-abasement as well". It was only after such utter and complete sense of failure with the upper classes that the missionaries, at long last, turned to the lower classes. This is how one of them put it: "I began with my eyes upon large towns and cities, but have been led from them to the county villages. I began with the educated classes and people of good social position, but ended up among the poor and lowly" (Gordon, p. 446). Even more revealing are the words of A.P. Mission Report of 1903. This was after 69 years of failure with the upper classes. Referring to "the proud and resisting high castes" the report said, "Here there is a strange absence of harvest .... There has arisen a belief that it is perhaps not God's will that the higher castes should be reached at this stage" (p. 33). So utterly complete was the failure of Christianity with better classes of society that, there was no other way of explaining it than by ascribing it to the will of God. Thus it was that, Christianity having almost completely failed with the upper classes finally became almost exclusively embedded in lower classes. This has naturally endowed Christianity with an image as not only a foreign religion but also a religion of the virtually excluded of society. In other words, the image of Christianity that has persisted in the minds of non-Christians of the sub-continent is that of a religion worthy only of the low and inconsequential section of society. It is not hard to see therefore that both Christianity and Christians suffer from a persistent image problem—a negative image elements of which are so historical in nature that they cannot be eradicated with any ease though, perhaps, can be neutralized to a certain degree.

These are then some of the background elements in the overall socio-historical situation of Christians in Pakistan. We now discuss other factors which have more current relevance. The state of the present Christian community may be summarized in these key words: small, weak, insufficiently protected, wanting in internal unity, devoid of effective leadership, and lacking in socio-cultural integration in the national fabric.

At best, there are 1.9% Christians in Pakistan. This dauntingly small proportionality is not only severe but is for ever and ever, and clearly points to an irredeemable weakness of the Christian community. Since politics is a game of numbers, it is not hard to see that Christians in Pakistan will always be a relatively powerless small minority. Originally, minorities in Pakistan were to be regarded as "**a sacred trust**" and, thus, were given a solemn promise of protection and promotion. But this was then and now is not then. Then was a promise of nothing short of a secular democracy in the land. The reality now is an Islamic state with legal and constitutional limits placed on all non-Muslims. The religious environment has thrown minorities open to abuse and suppression by ill informed and small-minded Muslim elements in society. Obviously, such societal elements are encouraged in their anti-minority behavior by the inability, or unwillingness, of the Government's law and order agencies to move against them firmly and effectively.

When a small and weak minority is deprived of full and effective protection by the powers that be, two consequences naturally follow: One, the mal factors in society assume a free range for their nefarious activities against the vulnerable minorities; and two, the fears and apprehensions of minorities are never put to rest but rather continue to multiply. It is not being suggested that Pakistan has failed to protect the Christian minority. What is being suggested is that, the protection provided has been mostly "reactive". What has been largely lacking is the "pro-active" measures with effective and prompt enforceability. For instance, let us consider the Blasphemy Law. This law is totally one-sided and unjust, and violates the Constitutional provision of "equality in the Law". A Muslim can so easily charge a Christian with blasphemy against Islam but a Christian has no legal ability of charging a Muslim for blaspheming against his religion. This is clearly lopsided justice without any tenable rationale whatsoever. When a Muslim chooses to charge a Christian with blasphemy, the case assumes a prima fascia character. But if a Muslim blasphemes against Christian religion, it usually goes un-noticed. Even the most elementary principle of justice requires that there be equality of treatment before the Law. Similarly, the Hudood Ordinances are an anathema to reasonability and tenets of modern law and principles of common justice.

Internally, the Christian minority is marked by a serious lack of unity and cohesion. In the first place the community is sharply divided into Protestants and Roman Catholics. These two groups have never been able to make serious common cause. This obviously weakens the Christian demand for effective protection. The Protestants are further divided into several denominations and splinter groups each concerned with its own narrow religious interests.

Additionally, there is a sickening lack of effective communal leadership. The main reason appears to be a sad confusion between the sociological concept of community and the religious concept of "church" or "Church community'. Obviously, in the strict sense, a church community encompasses only one direct aspect of the shared life of a human group whereas the sociological concept encompasses all aspects of the common or shared life of a group. Under this confusion of Church and community, many Church leaders presume to be community (secular) leaders as well. The idea being that if they are capable of providing leadership in religious affairs why can't they, as "pastors" or "keepers of the flock" do the same in secular affairs? Thus, there is always a tussle between the self-assuming clergy and the promising laymen who try to be the secular voice of the community. In Pakistan, this conflict has become quite ugly. The situation is like this: When the foreign Missions left the area, they left behind many large churches and attached lands and buildings. They also left behind many Christian schools and colleges that had been built on considerable real estate. Similarly, the Mission hospitals, with their ancillary buildings and grounds, and large missionary residences with attached lands, made up very large and attractive properties throughout the span of the land. Together they formed a very large source of real wealth. The local Church organizations, and prominent clergy, now have virtual possession of these properties. There is evidence to show that some of the clergy and their associates have acted in bad faith and have quietly sold off some of these properties at basement bargain prices, and have self-appropriated the proceeds. These and such other autocratic actions on the part of some of the senior clergy have naturally created deep divisions within the Church community. Consequently, with so many splinter groups, and so many diverse individuals claiming to be the leaders, it appears that Christians in Pakistan today are more of a "collectivity" and much less of a "community". There are hardly any well defined communal goals. There is hardly any "acceptable" leadership. And there is hardly any effective community organization. In fact, turf wars and factional strives are common which have left the community divided, weak, and ineffectual, both internally and externally.

The lack of effective secular leadership is the greatest weakness of the Christian minority in Pakistan. Presently, perhaps, clergy leadership in secular affairs may be a necessity. But, in the long run, Christians of Pakistan will need well groomed secular leadership. It is clear that, a rivalry between the clergy and the aspiring lay leadership has left the community badly divided. Thus, it appears that, an absence of strong community organization and effective leadership has rendered the community ineffectual in every respect.

The last part of the negative image of Christianity and Christians in Pakistan is perhaps, in the view of this writer, the most serious. And that is the lack of integration of Christians into the socio-cultural milieu of the land. The Christianity planted in Pakistan is clearly of a Western version of it. In this version, it exists as thoroughly abstracted, too deeply theologized, and much too much mythicalized. For a cultural area where people's understanding of religion is purely prescriptional and concretely situational, deep abstractions have but little relevance. For nearly a hundred and fifty years now, Christianity has existed in this area as it was brought here by its Western sponsors, i.e. too highly theologized and too abstractly argued. And for hundred and fifty years, it has remained a foreign religion in its tone and texture. It has failed to strike local roots and, therefore, is still looked upon as a foreign religion planted by foreigners during the sub-

Continent's time of foreign subjugation. A version of Christianity seeped in local idiom and local images, and compatible with the local experiences of the people will have to be developed if Christianity is to gain real roots in the Pakistani soil. In other words, planted by foreigners, and continuing in its foreign ways, Christianity remains largely a foreign religion. Nothing has been done to give it a local or indigenous shape. The style of worship continues to be Western; and the theological constructs imported from the West continue to represent the public face of Christianity. Talk to any Muslim about Christianity, and soon you will hear him referring to it as a Western implant with little congruence with local realities or cultural forms. A Christianity specially suited for being practiced in an Islamic environment will have to be developed if it is to be relevant to its context. In short, what is most important for the vitality of Christianity (and Christians) is its contextual shape and relevance. In other words, Christianity in Pakistan must have a Pakistani face.

As matters stand, Christians of Pakistan are fated to live their lives as a tiny and weak minority in a strident Islamic environment. Based on the world history of the two religions, and the pre-Christianity relations between the two communities as "haves" and "have-nots" of the Indian subcontinent, this environment will always be laced with a certain distantness if not outright alienation between the two communities. Depending on the degree of their religiosity, Muslims are likely to remain prone to be exclusionary towards Christians. Perhaps one might say that, so long as Pakistan remains a religious state, some elements of constraint against Christians are bound to remain. Under the circumstances, Christians have hardly any real choice but to work towards the widest possible accommodation between themselves and the Islamism that engulfs them. Under the circumstances, the only life possible for them is a life under some degree of Islamism. This reality is inalterable. It is, therefore, that we, once again, solemnly remind Christians of Pakistan of the Punjabi saying: 'A water dweller can hardly afford to be at odds with the crocodile'. If the tiny and powerless Christian minority wants to survive in Pakistan with any degree of normalcy, it has hardly any existential choice but to adjust to the Islamic environment that surrounds it so absolutely.

SIX

The Christian Future in Pakistan: Challenges and Choices

Thus far we have traced the origin, development, and the present situation of the Christian minority in Pakistan. Also, an attempt has been made to identify the different dimensions of what may be called the "Christian Problem" in Pakistan. In the present chapter, an attempt will be made to suggest ways and means for the Christian minority to meet the challenges inherent in their situation. Some of the proposals may sound capitulatory. In this connection, we must recall a Punjabi saying: "When you are decidedly weak, pre-accepting defeat and avoiding a face-off is the smartest thing to do". Or, when one suffers from comparative weakness, it is always more helpful to accept this fact beforehand than to pretend or to act otherwise. The more you "act" big the worse gets your position. Further, being noisy and confrontational gets one heard but hardly produces any positive results. In fact, too much protesting wins one the proverbial title of a "cry baby". It is always wiser to follow the path of quiet persuasion through reasoning and charm. Honey is always preferable to vinegar. Loud complaints may temporarily relieve frustration but, in the end they only add to one's grief. Christians in Pakistan, as a resource-less tiny minority, have no choice but to use patience and prudence in finding "realistic" solutions to their problems.

By way of reiterating the Christian problem in Pakistan, we note that the Christian minority in Pakistan is woefully small—at best less than 2% of the population. Originally, a part of it was drawn from the traditionally low stratum of society. Therefore, a background stigma continues to haunt <u>all</u> Christians to this day. Further, the brand of Christianity bequeathed to Christians by foreign Missions was, and continues to be, of a fundamentalist kind which creates its own problems.[1] During the early history of their existence, Christians of Pakistan were totally under the sway of the foreign missionaries whose idea of building a Church was to extract converts from their indigenous milieu and to confine them to an exclusively Christian compact. This fact produced a measurable estrangement between Christians and their indigenous environment. Of course It was natural for Missions to have spent their best efforts on the maximum Christianization of those who came into their fold, even to the clear detriment of their indigenous socio-cultural rootedness. Consequently, there was very little concern with the secular development of new Christians. With this single spiritual emphasis, the converted Christians turned into an "abstracted" part of society, with a separate collective life,

---

[1] It is my opinion that a fundamentalist Christianity is necessarily combative, non-conciliatory and rejectionist in nature and, therefore, clearly detrimental to the survival needs of a tiny minority, such as the Christians of Pakistan.

and their own foreign-affected sub-culture. Obviously, with this kind of extraneous-ness, whatever small part they might have had in their indigenous milieu was lost. To this day, Christians in Pakistan exist at the margins of society.

Another part of the Christian problem is the foreign appearance of Christian religion. From the tall Church steeples, to the polished wooden pews, to the pipe organ music, to the Western mode of worship, to a laughable pretence at being the "new Israel" and self-arrogating the stories of the Hebrew Bible to themselves, everything has a foreign-ness about it. Or interpreting the words of Jesus meant purely for the ears of Israelites of His day as somehow addressed to them, cannot be taken as anything other than pure fantasizing. For all practical purposes, Christianity in Pakistan is, and continues to remain, an alien reality. Thus, to the extent that the face of Christianity has continued to look foreign, it has remained difficult for Muslims to accept it as a local reality.

Further, the extremist religious climate in Pakistan appears to breed a serious level of intolerance which, when flares up, leads to all kinds of vilification, aggression, and even blatant breaches of Christians' civil and personal rights. The Blasphemy Law [Appendix C] is an easy tool for the intolerant and rogue elements to oppress members of the weak Christian minority. As soon as a Muslim chooses to charge a Christian with Blasphemy, the Christian in taken into protective custody (which means harsh jail-like conditions) for fear that an enraged Muslim zealot might kill the Christian before the courts have had a chance to hear out the case. The accused continues to rot in jail while the snail-paced justice system takes its own sweet time to bring it to conclusion. [Most judges are scared for their own lives at the hands of Muslim zealots and, therefore, keep putting off the case indefinitely, in the hope that religious hysteria might die down. One judge has actually been murdered by Muslim zealots]. There have been hundreds of unsuspecting Christians who, over the three decades of the Blasphemy law, have been falsely charged by Muslims either to display power, to oppress, or to extract undue advantage. The life of a few has been in such serious jeopardy that they had to be whisked out of the country. Others have been forced to pay "ransom" in one form or another to get the Muslim accusers off their backs.

A quite frequent form of oppression of Christians is the abduction of Christian females, even as young as thirteen, and their confinement for sexual purposes, or committal to brothels.[2] Some are coerced to convert to Islam. Thus Christians of Pakistan live in a state of perpetual fear of aggression, breach of their personal rights, and a haunting sense of vulnerability.

Under these circumstances, Christians of Pakistan will be well advised to develop keen sensibilities for the "realities" of their life. As they are less than two per cent of the population, it is quite obvious that their national status will always remain that of a very small minority. As such, their share of the economic resources of the nation will always be relatively small. Opportunities that may provide economic

---

[2] Early in 2009, in a rural area, a Muslim carried away a young Christian girl, raped her, and then confined her. When the poor father of the girl reported the matter to the police, the two brothers of the abductor came to his house, and in the hearing of all the neighbors told him: 'If you do not withdraw the police complaint, we promise you your other two girls (who were only 10 and 12 then) will meet a worse fate. The poor father mulled over the prospects, and finally withdrew the complaint. Did he have any other choice?

advancement will not come their way easily. Similarly, State provided educational and training opportunities that may improve their economic abilities will not be easily available to them. Above all, as a small minority, their ability to influence the political processes (in an Islamic Theocracy) will always be highly limited if not non-existent. In short, under the circumstances as they prevail, Christians will always be open to economic handicap, social exclusion, and political insignificance. Secondly, unless the Christian religion sheds its foreign-ness and takes on an indigenous shape and coloring, its respect in the eyes of the dominant Muslim majority will remain limited. Thirdly, unless Christians develop effective integration into the socio-cultural milieu of the land, they will remain subject to the processes of marginalization. Finally, so long as Islamism remains the "essential" and all-pervasive reality in Pakistan, Christians of Pakistan will have no choice but to learn to adapt to this overwhelming reality as best as they can. With these as the "givens" of the Christian situation in Pakistan, we suggest some goals and objectives, both internal and external, which Christians should pursue in order to become a more meaningful part of their milieu.

To the Christian purists, some of the suggestions for "internal reform" might appear extreme. But no apologies are offered. The nature of Christian situation in Pakistan clearly demands novel measures for its alleviation including, what may be called, the practice of a predominantly "contextual Christianity". It is high time that Christians of Pakistan grew up and realized that Pakistan is an Islamic country with an Islamic Constitution, an Islamic Law, and an Islamic Government. Life in Pakistan is possible only as it can be lived in adjustment to these irreducible realities. Clearly, the one most crucial reality surrounding Christians is the religion of Islam. Therefore, life in Pakistan (for a religious minority) is possible only in as much as it can be lived in reconciliation with Islam. All other views and attitudes are unrealistic, short-sighted, and even self-defeating, and will result in nothing but further dwarfing of the life of the Christian minority. Therefore, at this stage of our discussion, we ask the question: **Given the nature of Pakistan, what is the most realistic future for Christians in Pakistan? Are there ways of making this future more meaningful?** Do Christians of Pakistan wish to live a securer and more satisfying life, or are they content with a life of exclusion and marginality? Assuming the former to be the only real answer, and the ultimate goal of Christians, I suggest the pursuit of the following measures:

It appears that the overall goal of the Christian community must be to become an integral part of the Pakistani society. All the known factors considered, this appears to be the most important goal to pursue. So long as the Christians in Pakistan remain content to exist at the margins of society, their image as an extraneous entity will continue to stand. In other words, Christianity and Christians will have to so transform themselves as to become every bit a Pakistani reality, so that even those Muslims who may wish to consider them as extraneous may find it hard to do so. For such a transformation, Christians will have to take some drastic steps, both external and internal. In this regard, some of the proposals and suggestions made hereunder will appear extreme to the religionist Christians of Pakistan. However, given the nature of the situation, Christians have no other constructive choice. Some truly bold and dramatic measures are called for if meaningful change is to be achieved.

A purist or absolutist Christianity is laudable but may not always be possible under certain circumstances. A true and honest examination of the Christian situation in Pakistan demands measures that will override some of the problems associated with the brand of Christianity which may be called "fundamentalist", "mission-loaded" or "expansionist". I dare to assert that, the only real and viable choice available to Christians in Pakistan is to develop and follow two-directional Christianity—externally "situational"[3] and internally "liberal" with Islam-reconciliation as the central motivation. This is to say that, given the nature of Pakistan, the only Christianity that is ultimately realizable is an Islam-adjusted Christianity[4]. It is as obvious as obvious can be that, Christians do not have the ability now, nor are they likely to have it any time in the future, to alter the Islamic situation in which they find themselves. Article 2 of the Constitution of Pakistan reads: "Islam shall be the State Religion of Pakistan and the injunctions of Islam as laid down in the Holy Qur'an and Sunnah shall be the supreme Law and source of guidance for legislation to be administered through the Laws enacted by the Parliament and Provincial Assemblies and for policy making by the Government". So long as Islam holds sway in the land, traditional Christianity and Christians in Pakistan will be under pressure in some form or manner. Under the circumstances, the challenge facing the Christian minority is how best to adjust to the Islamic situation in order to live a maximally safe, secure, and

---

[3] "Situational Christianity" is that Christianity the practice of which is maximally cognizant of the environmental factors impinging on it.

[4] By "Islam-adjusted Christianity" we simply mean a version of Christianity that lays more stress on those aspects of Christianity which are relatively more acceptable to Muslims and privatizes the issues that have been conflict-producing over the last thirteen centuries.

satisfying life. Let it be said once again that, while the hope for unfettered democracy in Pakistan cannot be abandoned, the concrete realities of here and now must be faced squarely. In this regard, there are certain measures, both external and internal, which appear essential for Christians to pursue as diligently as possible. Some of these goals and objectives have been discussed below, but only by way of suggestions. No claim is made as to their exclusivity or finality.

Internally, the most glaring problem of the Christian community in Pakistan is the absence of effective **secular leadership.**[5] Right now what best describes the Christian situation in Pakistan is the American saying: "too many chiefs, few Indians". The fact that there are too many (self-styled) leaders is not necessarily bad. It only proves that there are many individuals who are keenly concerned about the wellbeing of the community and want to see something done. But obviously too many cooks spoil the broth. What is needed most is the establishment of a single **central leadership** that can inspire the trust and confidence of a cross section of the community. Otherwise the affairs of the community will always remain in disarray.

However, a prerequisite to any successful communal leadership is the development of **clearly defined and achievable communal goals.** But before there is any talk of goals, there has to be a sufficient communal **unity.** (One reinforces the other). Christians in Pakistan are badly factionalized and divided into sundry groups. The major and worst division is between Protestants and Roman Catholics. The

---

[5] We cannot emphasize too much the need for a separation between religious matters and secular matters. The mixing of two has been nonproductive thus far and, in our estimation, will remain so in the future too.

community is split right down the middle. Consequently, there is no one consistent Christian voice in the land. This dividedness is obviously detrimental to Christian communal interests. While the realization of this internal division is generally present in the community, unfortunately nothing has succeeded in eradicating it. Something very drastic, even impositional in nature, needs to be done in order to bring about the much needed Christian communal unity of purpose and action.[6] It is clear that competitive leadership has proven ineffectual and, in fact, has created much of the current divisiveness that so widely prevails. It is high time, therefore, that Pakistani Christians submitted to a "collective leadership". In this regard, the creation and establishment of a secular body called the **Christian Community Leadership Council** (or something akin to it) is proposed. This Council, hereafter referred to as CCLC, should be the sole voice of the Christian community in **all secular matters.** (Church/ecclesiastic matters shall be essentially outside the purview of this Council). Its overall function should be to produce unity of thought and action in socio-cultural and political matters, and to provide enlightened leadership in all matters of community safety, security, and development.

It is hard to devise a precise method for the creation of the proposed Leadership Council except to suggest that a few concerned and self-less individuals should take matters into their own hands and work toward the creation of this Council.[7] We suggest that It be composed of roughly

---

[6] No brief as to the union of Roman Catholics and Protestants is offered. I am sure, however, that this is not as great a problem as it appears. Given the will and the imagination, the problem is resolvable.

twenty-four well educated and well regarded persons from both Catholic and Protestant sections of the community— four from Baluchistan, four from NWFP, six from Sind (including two from Karachi), and ten from Punjab (no more than two from Lahore). The method of delegation to this body (election or nomination) should be up to each of the four provinces. The term of service should be three or four years on a rotating basis. One member from each province should retire every three years to be replaced by a new member from that province. The retiring members may be renominated/re-elected at the discretion of the Council. A representative of the World Council of Churches, and a similar representative of the Catholic Church, should be ex-officio members of this Council. This Council should serve as the community leadership body. Its major function should be the formulation and pursuance of **all secular goals and concerns** of the Christian community. It is proposed that there be only three officers of this Council—chair, vice chair, and executive secretary. They should hold offices for no more than three years at a time. These positions should be held on alternating basis between Catholic and Protestant members aspiring to them. The chair of the Council should be the only spokesperson of the organization, and his opinions should reflect the collective mind of the Council. The major functions of this Leadership Council should be: (1) to formulate community developmental policies and programs (long term and short term), in socio-economic, educational, and political fields; (2) to make representation

---

[7] Perhaps Pakistan Christian Council (with appropriate Roman Catholic participation) can act as host in this matter. They could judiciously put together a group of four or five self-less individual who should get the ball rolling toward the establishment of the said leadership body (CCLC).

to the Government of Pakistan, and other national and international bodies, as needed; (3) to keep liaison with international bodies and organizations having an interest in the protection and promotion of the Christian minority in Pakistan; (4) to devise ways and means for unifying the community into one cohesive whole; and (5) to promote ways and means by which Christians may attain maximum integration into the national milieu. The Leadership Council should be a registered body with its head office in Islamabad or Lahore.

In the view of this writer, among the first concerns of this Leadership Council should be to seek international recognition for the Christians of Pakistan as an "insufficiently protected minority". The United Nations Organization has reserved the nomenclature of "persecuted minorities" only for those minorities whose persecution is "open", "systemic" and state-sponsored in nature. Since Christian suffering in Pakistan takes place at the hands of private actors, they cannot be designated as a "persecuted minority". Thus the US State Department and other international organizations have chosen to use the designation of "insufficiently protected" minority for the Christians of Pakistan. However, since the consequences of "insufficient protection" can be just as ominous as the consequences of state-condoned persecution, a case must be made at the UNO for the creation of a new official category i.e. "insufficiently protected minorities". Given the overall situation, and the clear and ongoing potential for Christian minority to be subjected to continuing oppressive acts, one of the urgent tasks of the CCLC should be to make a case at the UNO for the "international recognition" of the Pakistani Christian minority as an "insufficiently protected" minority. We reiterate that the differentiation between "open and systematic persecution and non-systematic but persistent persecution" is completely artificial since the consequences of one can be as devastating as of the other. The differentiation is, therefore, tantamount to hair-splitting.

In any event, since most acts of aggression are committed against isolated, less educated, and poorer members of the Christian community who are not only ignorant of the complexities of the justice system but are usually lacking in the means of affording the legal costs. It is proposed, therefore, that CCLC build and operate a **Christian legal Defense Fund.** That, in the building of this fund, while there may be assistance from international Church bodies, local Pakistani Christians must play a major role. There are at least one million Christian families in Pakistan. Even if each family contributes only one rupee per year toward this fund, there will be a floating fund of one million rupees on hand each year to fight the court battles against cases of discrimination and charges of blasphemy. It will be up to CCLC to devise a method for the collection and disbursement of this fund. With the availability of this fund, the CCLC will be in a position to appoint/hire top notch lawyers in each district city to be always available for the legal defense of Christians who are being harassed, oppressed, or persecuted under Blasphemy Law or for any other unjust or discriminatory reason.

Further, the Leadership Council should seek some necessary **amendments to the Constitution** of Pakistan in order to make it more protective of the interests of the Christian minority. This recommendation is made with the clear realization that Christian minority's political capital is too insignificant. Therefore, persuading the powers that be to move on this issue will not be easy. However, with quiet but firm persistence, and with the help of the concerned international organizations, the Government of Pakistan may be persuaded to make the needed amendments to the Constitution:

The first proposed amendment pertains to the "Objectives Resolution" which occupies a pivotal position in the Constitutional of Pakistan. Christians of Pakistan would be well advised to seek the following amendments to the Resolution: Paragraph four (Article 2A) should be amended to read: "Wherein the principles of democracy, freedom, equality, tolerance and social justice as enunciated by Islam for Muslims, and as set forth internationally for religious minorities shall be fully observed".

In paragraph six, the qualifier "freely" should be re-inserted to make it true to the original version of the Objectives Resolution: "Wherein adequate provisions shall be made for minorities "freely"[8] to practice their religion and develop their cultures".

In paragraph nine, the un-defined term "legitimate" should be removed by making the paragraph to read: "Wherein adequate provisions shall be made to safeguard the religious, economic, political, social, and cultural interests of recognized minorities and depressed classes as equal citizens of Pakistan". It should be obvious that, when a minority is recognized as legitimate, all of its social, cultural, economic, religious, and political interests automatically become legitimate and should be regarded as such.

Article 19 of the Constitution, regarding **Freedom of Speech,** reads: "Every citizen shall have the right to free-

---

[8] The qualifier "freely" was included in the original constitution and in subsequent constitutions excepting the present constitution where it is conspicuous by its absence.

dom of speech and expression, and there shall be freedom of the press, subject to any reasonable restrictions imposed by Law in the interest of the glory of Islam or the integrity, security or defense of Pakistan or any part thereof, friendly relations with foreign states, public order, decency or morality, or in relation to contempt of Court, (commission of) or incitement to an offence". The right to freedom of speech is granted, but has been placed under as many as seven restrictions, including "the interest of glory of Islam". This restriction clearly constitutes an injustice to the religious minorities. While public order and common decency demand of Christians that they be respectful towards Islam as the State-religion, and also as a world religion of consequence, their speech cannot be subjected to the "glorification" of Islam. Non-Muslims can certainly be expected to accord respect and deference to the State Religion, but cannot be made to "glorify" it through a constitutional requirement.

Article 33 deals with five kinds of prejudice. It reads: "The State shall discourage parochial, racial, tribal, sectarian and provincial prejudice among the citizens". But the most pernicious kind of prejudice, i.e. the religious prejudice, is conspicuous by its absence. Christians should diligently seek an amendment to have religious prejudice explicitly included as the sixth prejudice under this clause of the Constitution.

Article 37 of the Constitution relates to promotion of social justice and eradication of social evils. The fourth provision under this Article reads: "The State shall ensure inexpensive and expeditious justice". Because of the admittedly very slow moving justice system of Pakistan, the pursuit of justice for most members of the Christian minority is so highly cumbersome and draining of their financial and emotional resources that, by the time it is delivered, the persons concerned have already suffered devastating emotional and financial consequences. Therefore, Article 37, Clause (d) should be amended to read: "The State shall ensure inexpensive and expeditious justice for all but shall make special provisions for minorities and persons of low economic means".

A high priority should be accorded by Community Leadership Council to the repeal of the **Blasphemy Law.** Christians, with the help of the international community, have been trying for years to have the Government of Pakistan repeal this very regressive and anti-minority law. The problem for the Government of Pakistan seems to be that they do not appear to have any other means of suppressing what they see as the Ahmadia heresy except by means of a law such as the Blasphemy Law. The specific problem for Christians presented by this law is that, it is blatantly one-sided. While Christians have been made punishable for blaspheming against Islam, Muslims have been left free to blaspheme against Christianity at will. Obviously, the Law, as it exists, is totally one-sided. Therefore, it is proposed that, if the Blasphemy Law must stay, it be amended in such a way as to be equitable to all world religions recognized by Islam. Hereunder we propose a possible form of it:

Proposed Law Regarding Injury to Religious Feelings and Sentiments
(To replace present Blasphemy Law)

Islam, and all other faiths recognized by Islam, shall be accorded due respect and honor by all citizens of Pakistan, and by others present in Pakistan. Therefore, persons committing acts, gestures, signs, imputations, innuendos, insinuations with conscious and willful intent to demean, dishonor, ridicule, trivialize, or to engage in verbal abuse or denigration of such religions, their founders, their holy books, their high personages, or their followers shall be liable for prosecution and, if found guilty in a regular court of law, shall be punishable by fine, imprisonment, or both, at the discretion of the court.

Membership in National Assembly and the Senate: As presently constituted, there are ten seats reserved for non-Muslims in a total body of three hundred and forty-two of the National Assembly. This is obviously a token of Islamic good will towards minorities. It would serve Pakistan's image much better if this token was enlarged to make it a little more meaningful by raising it to sixteen—five Hindus and Sikhs (almost exclusively residing in the province of Sindh); five Christian ; five Ahmadias; and one from other minorities. In practical term, this will still be no more than a token. But it will be relatively a more respectable token. The same goes for the Senate. "Recognized" minorities must have a voice in the Senate, however small that voice might be. The present Prime Minister, Yousuf Raza Gilani, recognized the anomaly of having reserved seats for minorities in the National Assembly but none in the Senate and, on December 16, 2008, told the officials at the Ministry of Minority Affairs that there would be five reserved seats for minority representatives in the Senate. But minorities do not feel that there is much chance of this promise coming to fruition for the next Senate election in 2012. The present is an ill-logical situation in that, while there are reserved seats for minorities in the House, there is no such seat in the Senate. This anomaly must be rectified.

Also, the proposed Leadership Council must pursue a change in the **Oath of Office** of the President, Prime Minister, Governors of Provinces, and the Chief Ministers of Provinces. Paragraph 7 of these oaths as set forth in the Constitution reads: "That, in all circumstances, I will do right to all manner of people, according to Law, without fear or favor, affection or ill will". The phrase "all manner of people" appears to be too imprecise. It is proposed, therefore, that a specific reference to religious minorities be included in the Oath thusly: "That, in all circumstances, I will do right to all manner of people, especially the recognized religious minorities, according to Law, without fear or favor, affection or ill will". As an Islamic State, avowing to be democratic, Pakistan must make sure that it is prepared to protect the interests of religious minorities in every possible way.

Further, the proposed CCLC should, work towards the establishment of an **Office of Minority Relations.** Established through an act of Parliament, this Office should be under the patronage of the President of Pakistan. Composed of equal number of progressive minds from both Muslim and minority communities, this board should serve as the official watchdog for the maintenance and promotion of quality relations between minority communities and Muslims. It should work diligently toward developing national policies and programs aimed at bringing about closer relations between national minorities and Muslims in the cities as well as the county side. The presence of such an Office will stand as a permanent reminder to those elements in society who appear to disregard the "sacred" duty of the ruling majority towards the well-being of the law-abiding, peaceable, and contributive minorities.

It might also serve the Christian community well to exploit the services of Pakistani Christians living abroad. It is proposed, therefore, that the CCLA create a special core of appropriate Christian individuals living abroad (Europe, North America, etc.) called the "**Concerned Individuals Abroad**". As the name implies, the function of these individuals will be to make sure that their respective governments abroad are kept fully apprised of the true situation of Christians in Pakistan and to urge them to use their good offices to promote the safety and security of Christian minority in Pakistan. We realize that international aid that so freely flows into Pakistan is officially without strings attached. Yet we are convinced that, if there was the will of tying aid to the question of measureable protection and general well-being of minorities, ways will be found to accomplish this end without much difficulty. Perhaps foreign aid to Pakistan is already related to the protection of minorities. If it is, making this fact public knowledge will go a long way towards enhancing the sense of security of minorities in Pakistan.

One of the most serious problems facing Christians in Pakistan, which is becoming more and more pressing every day, is the forced, coerced, or otherwise contrived marriage of Muslim men to Christian women. Islam does not allow Muslim women to marry Christian men unless the men first convert to Islam. However, Muslim men are allowed to take Christian wives whether they convert to Islam or remain Christian. Once a Christian woman is taken as wife she loses the right of divorce because, in Islam, only men have the right to divorce. This creates a very anomalous situation.

This situation becomes a lot worse if children are involved. Islamic law is blatantly male oriented. Even where it is clear that the children's best interests will be served if they remain in the custody of the mother, they are usually committed to the custody of the Muslim fathers. It is obvious that a Muslim court would, among other things, consider Islamic influence of the father to be in the best interest of the child. Further, even when children are committed to the custody of the Christian mother, the mother can be subjected to all kinds of harassment and harm in order for her to concede custody to the Muslim father. Under the circumstances, there is a dire need for an interfaith marriage act in Pakistan which will be just and equitable to both parties, and which, in case of divorce, will be clearly oriented towards the best interests of the children and the mother.

Christian girls, as young as thirteen or fourteen, are being sexually abused with the connivance of Muslim clergy, with the leniency of Muslim police, and with the sympathy of Muslim judges. Many a time, this is done in the pious sounding name of marriage. Muslim men abduct, lure, or otherwise trap young Christian girls, and sexually use and abuse them. The reasons for this are clear: Christians are poor and weak, and can easily be preyed upon. The laws to protect them are utterly inadequate. And the law enforcement personnel (Muslim) are often prone to be insensitive to their cause.

Considering the overwhelming odds against Christians, one way of dealing with this situation would be to regularize sexual relations between Christians and Muslims by passing an equitable **Interfaith Marriage Act.** As matters stand today, Islam allows Muslim men to marry Christian women. But Christian men may not marry Muslim women without first converting to Islam. Without getting into an elaborate discussion of the issues involved, let it be acknowledged that this problem is not only serious but is likely to get worse unless a reasonable and just solution is instituted at an early date; a solution which would be fair, equitable, and reasonably workable under the given situation in Pakistan.

It is proposed, therefore, that, under an initiative of the CCLA, an interfaith body be set up to thrash out and propose to the Government a comprehensive interfaith marriage act. This body should be composed of equal number of members from all faith communities, and should include clergy, social scientists, law professionals, and legislators.

The idea of interfaith marriage when presented to the traditionalist Christians, often draws a strong protest. The argument advanced goes like this: Christians are relatively poor and generally lower on the social prestige scale. As such, a Christian woman marrying a Muslim man would be marrying up and attaining a higher social status for herself, her children, and her close relatives. If Christian-Muslim marriage comes to have legal sanction, many poor Christian women, consciously or unconsciously, will be tempted to seek it because of its prestige raising value. This will be clearly detrimental to the interests of the Christian community. To this purely sentimental argument, there is a strong countervailing realistic argument—Under the Pakistani circumstances, inter-religious sexual contacts are unavoidable and are bound to increase as time passes on. There is no other way of regularizing them and/or legally protecting the interest of the weaker party, i.e. the Christian women. Obviously, if Christian women have sufficient grounding in their own religion, and have pride in their own community, they will think twice before entering into any such cross-religious sexual relationships. But what if they get lured or trapped, or get genuinely involved with Muslim males? After all there are some natural human urges that affect such situations. In the ultimate analysis inter-sex contacts between Christians and Muslims in Pakistan are an inevitability. And the rate of such contacts is bound to increase with the passage of time.[9] Opposing it on emotional grounds will not help. The best approach to this problem, therefore, is to provide as much legal protection to the weaker party, i.e. the Christian women, as possible. This can be done only in the framework of a Marriage Act which can provide all the possible and necessary safeguards.

At the attitudinal level, the most urgent need is the elimination of all remnants of a blatantly negative Christian attitude towards Islam and Muslims. The Scriptural commandments of **love your neighbor as yourself,** or **judge not that you be not judged, for you will be judged just as you judge others,** or **see not the speck in another's eye when there is log in your own** were never more relevant than for Christians of Pakistan. The ingrained Christian negativity towards Islam and Muslims is an internal poison which is eating up Christians. This poison must be extracted at all costs. Christians must realize that Muslims are more than their "neighbors". The two are inheritors of the same homeland; and the fate of the one is the fate of the other. Therefore, we propose that, the CCLC undertake an intense program of **attitude reform** towards Islam and Muslims. From Sunday pulpit sermons to local seminars and other communication means, Christians must be led to move towards the

---

[9] I personally know of a male Christian doctor who fell in love with a very nice and open-minded Muslim girl but, in the end, had to flee the county because of serious threats to his life from her folks.

development of a positive and constructive attitude towards Islam and Muslims. For ages, attitudinal negativity of one towards the other has been the hall mark of these two communities. It is only in the best interest of Christians to bring about the reform of this negativity. After all, love of neighbor is the greatest commandment given to Christians by their religion. There are no ifs and buts. Where there is love there is tolerance; where there is tolerance there is appreciation; and where there is appreciation there is greater bonding. Christians are called upon by their religion to adopt a positive attitude and loving disposition toward even their enemies. Muslims are no enemies; they are almost like kith and kin and sharers of a common life. Then why should there be any problem in developing positive and forbearing attitude towards them. Whenever this author has proposed to Christian friends the idea of developing positive attitude towards Muslims, the uniform answer has always been: 'It cannot be done because Muslims are so strongly negative towards us'. Are we to love only those who love us? Is that Christian love? We are commanded to love even those who hate us and wish us ill. Only love begets love. Unless Christians change their disposition towards Muslims, Muslims will have little reason to change their view of Christians.

When all is said and done, the developmental need of the community that still stands out as a sore thumb is for the elimination of its economic and occupational disability. The one factor which is most responsible for the negative image of the Christian community is the confinement of a part of it to the stigmatized occupation, the sanitation work. So long as even an insignificant part of the community remains in this occupation, the whole community will remain subject to this social stigma. There appears to be no magical formula to rid the community of this source of a negative image except the natural process of education and increased economic ability which will gradually lift this part of the community into relatively more respectable occupational life. We propose, therefore, that CCLC work for the establishment of a special fund for the education of promising youth from the down trodden Christian families. We realize the difficulties involved in a program of this nature. But what has to be done has to be done. There is no other choice in the matter. We are sure that the Leadership Council will be up to this task. It may be suggested that an **Education Aid Fund** be especially established for this purpose. As suggested above, if each Christian family in Pakistan were to donates one or two rupees a year towards this fund, there will be a floating fund of a million or two million rupees on hand for this purpose every year, earmarked for the education of slum children of Christian families.

Another essential need of the Christian community is to forge a strong **union between Roman Catholics and Protestants** in all matters but especially in the areas of communal solidarity and developmental pursuits. As matters stand today, in many ways these two groups act as rivals of one another. This is a short-sightedness that must come to an end. In countries where Christianity is the dominant religion, Christians can afford the luxury of dividing themselves into Protestants and Catholics. But, in a country where both put together are less than two percent of the population, this dividedness appears to be ludicrous. In Pakistan, there is a clear need for a strong union between Protestant and Roman Catholics. Theological differences will take a long time to resolve, if at all. But, in the meantime social and political unity appears to be an absolute necessity. In any event, the

Muslim majority sees all Christians as one entity. It is high time, therefore, that, in all socio-economic and political matters, Protestants and Catholics present themselves as one communal reality. It would be lamentable if, under the circumstances, the two did not act as one body in all social and political matters. Therefore, we recommend that, in order for a greater Christian solidarity in the land, the proposed CCLC work diligently towards a strong secular union, pulling together Christians of all kinds and all persuasions, irrespective of their theologies, into one single communal whole. Obviously, joint Catholic and Protestant communal programs would be the most impact making. But, if joint programs are not possible, coordinated operational policies would be the next best thing. What we are really proposing here is a collective approach to the development of a body of cohesive goals and purposes. Internal divisions, in this regard, are utterly unacceptable. These internal divisions should not be allowed to prevent Christians from presenting themselves as one family. It is an absolute imperative that Protestants and Roman Catholics make one common cause in Pakistan, and join hands and minds as one single community with one common goal of life with dignity and security.

There is also the question of Christian Services in Pakistan. Originally these services were established as tools of Christian Missions. But in reality they proved to be pioneers in the fields of education, health, and certain welfare services. For over a hundred years, Christian schools and colleges provided first rate modern education to a cliental that was overwhelmingly non-Christian. In 1972, to please boisterous Islamism the Government of Pakistan nationalized most Christian schools and colleges. These schools and colleges have now been denationalized but most of them are in such a run down condition that the Presbyterian Church of America, the original owner of most institutions, is loath to take them back. Only those that were in rehabilitable shape have been taken over and are under the direct management and control of the American Presbyterian Church of America. In any event, the operational policy and management of these institutions bears no direct link to the local Christian community. Perhaps this best assures their safe continuation into the future. Strategically, there appears nothing wrong with this situation. But it does hurt the image of the local Christian community as lacking in ability or aptitude for a role in the management and operation of these institutions. To remove this anomaly, we propose that some mechanism be establishment by which the Pakistani Christian community may appear to be an important stakeholder in the delivery of all Christian services in Pakistan however foreign-created or foreign-operated those services may be. This will assuredly enhance the prestige of the national Pakistani Christian community. In this regard, we propose that CCLA create a body called **Christian Services Consultation Committee.** Twelve Pakistani Christians with high educational qualifications and proven vision (from within or outside of Pakistan) be nominated to this committee by the proposed Leadership Council with the consultation of the American Presbyterian Board of Education. As the name implies, the relationship of this committee to the American Presbyterian Board of Education shall be purely advisory in nature and will primarily comprise an annual consultation conference. Through this device, there will be a visible role of the national Christian community in the matter of national Christian services in Pakistan.

Next to smallness in numbers, the Christian minority in Pakistan is handicapped by its general **economic incapacity.** There is a much smaller minority in Pakistan called the Parsees. This minority has hardly a problem because they are economically among the elite of the land. It will be unfair to deny that, over the last fifty years, Christians have made progress in the economic realm but much more needs to be done if the image of Christians as the proverbial poor of the land is to be eradicated. We, therefore, suggest that one of the CCLC's foremost responsibilities should be to prepare a long-range plan for the industrial and commercial development of the community. Many Christian groups live in far flung and isolated parts of the country. Transportation and communication for these groups is a serious problem. But perhaps the non-availability of start-up capital is their most urgent need in terms of their industrial development. Starting small, therefore, is perhaps the only way forward. The age-old idea of "cottage industry" is perhaps the only idea that appears feasible under the circumstances. This author is not an economist. He can only point to the need. The systematic program planning in this area will have to be developed under the auspices of the proposed CCLC.

The idea of industrial development is essentially dependent on the availability of industrial skills within the community. We cannot say with any certainty, but it appears that, the level of such skills is badly wanting in the Christian community of Pakistan. The acquisition of industrial skills, therefore, remains one of the essential needs of the Christian community. Right now, we are aware of only two industrial schools, one in Gujranwala and the other in Karachi [under YMCA auspices] some eight hundred miles apart. Though the potential of these schools is high, their success rate for Christians leaves much to be desired. We, therefore, propose the creation of industrial schools across the land by converting some of the old schools/institutes (including those recovered from nationalization) into either full-time or part-time/evening industrial schools. It appears that there is a good potential for the start up of such schools/institutes all across the land. There are facilities in Karachi, Sukhar, Multan, Sahiwal, Gojra, Faisalabad, Lahore, Gujranwala, Sialkot, Gujrat, Rawalpindi, and Peshawar that can lend themselves, either fully or partially, for such conversion. In all these population centers, there are Christian communities, but more importantly, there are Christian properties that can be utilized for the development and promotion of Christian industrial schools. This author is personally aware of a Christian school in the prominent industrial city of Sialkot—the CTI High School—which is eminently suited for an evening industrial school. Since the physical structures are already there, what is required is organizational and operational capitol. Much of it will be derivable from the instructional fees. Obviously, the programs will be open to all parts of the population, i.e. Christians and Muslims, rich and poor. After all, Muslims are 96% of the population. Through out the history of Christian schools and colleges, non-Christians have been the major source of populating them. Christian schools and colleges were the pioneers in bringing liberal education to the sub-continent. It is high time they became the vanguard of industrial education. Of course the local Christian community is unable to take this initiative on its own. Unless the foreign Churches, involved in Christian services in Pakistan, adopt this priority, its realization will remain a pipe dream. In any event, we present this as a challenge to the proposed Christian Leadership Council.

However, after all is said and done, nothing will succeed until and unless Christians of Pakistan become an integral part of the Pakistani society and culture. As things stand, Christians exist at the margin of society and, therefore, are treated as such. This state of affairs has prevailed for too long now. Christians have continually been marked by socio-cultural "exclusion" and "marginality". They exist in the land but their impact on the societal processes amounts to very little. There is a hidden belief among Muslims, and also among some Christians of Pakistan that, Pakistan was created by Muslims, only for Muslims. That it is first and foremost the country of Muslims. No one else can have the level of stake in it as the Muslims do. All this may be true to a certain degree but cannot be the whole story. Nothing can erase the natural birth right of non-Muslims who have belonged to this land from times immemorial. Thus, under the circumstances, as they prevail today, the Christians in Pakistan are faced with the challenge of attaining maximum "belongingness". But this belongingness will always be proportional to their "accepted-ness" by Muslims. Similarly, accepted-ness is virtually impossible without a sufficient degree of "compatibility". So the highest challenge facing the Christians of Pakistan is to attain to a workable degree of amenability to Islam, both religiously and culturally.

SEVEN
Towards an Islam-
Reconciled Christianity

It is well known that, the first organized attempt at introducing Christianity into the Indian subcontinent was made by Jesuits missionaries during the Mughal period. It appears that while King Akbar may have had rather an open mind toward Christianity, the other Mughal kings were determinedly resistant to a possible Christian intrusion. In fact, as we have noted above, towards 1635, Shah Jehan, issued a final decree banning the conversion of Muslims to Christianity, and thus, revoking the earlier decree of 1601, issued by Akbar, which had permitted the conversion of Mughal subjects to Christianity. Shah Jehan made it a serious crime not only to seek Muslim conversion but also to agree to be converted. Thus, when Christianity finally arrived in India with the British Raj, the Muslim wall of resistance was already up and firmly in place. This Muslim wall has existed for centuries, and is likely to remain for the foreseeable future.

TOWARDS AN ISLAM-RECONCILED CHRISTIANITY

Under the circumstances, the only wise choice open to Christians of Pakistan is not to keep hoping and wishing for a change in Muslim disposition but to make the necessary creative adjustment to it as the next best option. In this regard, we propose the development and practice of a kind of Christianity which is not aggressively self-righteous and proud but is humble and is willing to make the necessary accommodations and adjustments. It goes without saying that, if the assertions of Christianity are unique, they ought to be self-recommending and self-sustaining. They should not be dependent upon any human promotion. There is an Urdu saying: Jadu woh jo sir char kar bolay, i.e. if it is true magic, it is bound to break all resistance to it. If there is true power in the claims of Christianity, it must be self-recommending, self-sustaining, and self-promoting. The kind of confrontational/evangelical Christianity that was brought to the Indian sub-continent by the West should become a thing of the past.

In my humble view, the circumstances in which Christians and Christianity find themselves in Pakistan today call for the development and practice of a *"conciliatory Christianity"* in stead of an aggressively evangelical Christianity That is, a Christianity the form and content of which is maximally compatible with the demands of the situation in which it finds itself. In Pakistan, this means the Islamic situation. I know the Christianists will bristle at this suggestion because it will jar their fundamentalist impulses. But when the only medicine that works is bitter, it should not be spared just because of its bitterness.

As we know, Islam has a peculiar relationship with Christianity. All other religions are so completely "other" that there is no difficulty in determining how to relate to them. But Islam presents a peculiar problem, in that, it accepts the direct teachings of Hazrat Issa Masih but is vehemently opposed to the doctrinal teachings of the Church[1].

Thus, we know that the roots of incompatibility between Christianity and Islam are not as much the direct teachings of Hazrat Issa Masih as they are due to the petrified doctrines of the Church. Under the circumstances, the most constructive choice for the Christians of Pakistan is to take positive steps towards closing this doctrinal gap and following the path of reconciliation with Islam and Muslims.

The Christians of Pakistan must shed all stereotypes of Islam and Muslims in an honest-to-God attempt at closing the division to the greatest possible degree. It is also obvious that, in the situation as it prevails in Pakistan, it is the Christians who need to take the initiative toward this process of reconciliation. And they must do so with all sincerity and without reserve. The attitude of why should a religion of higher sophistication reconcile with a religion of lesser sophistication is the most asinine and poisonously destructive. So far, this attitude has led to nothing but entrenched negativity between the two religions. In this day and age, it is of the utmost importance that Christians living in Islamic lands develop a positive disposition towards Islam and Muslims. It is high time for rapprochement and rapport. Estrangement and strife must come to an end. Both sides need to change, but it is the Christians who are commanded by "Christian love and humility" to undertake the initiative. This is not a matter of yielding one to the other; it is a matter of adaptive adjustment. But the movement toward one an-

---

[1] For Muslims, the most unacceptable aspects of Christianity are the Church created doctrines of Trinity and Expiation. (These doctrines are clearly outside the pale of Hazrat Issa Masih's direct teachings, and are the creation of the Church).

other will not be possible so long as Christians remain en-trenched in the practice of the old, absolutist, and "mission-ized"[2] Christianity. Such Christianity is, by its very nature, conflict loaded.

True Islam is basically accommodative and tolerant to-wards Christianity. The Holy Qur'an, in fact, commands a positive attitude towards non-believers. The whole of Surah 109 (Those Who Reject Faith) is a command from God, and reads: "O Prophet say to the deniers of Islam: O you Kafirs I do not worship those which you worship nor you worship the God that I worship. I say it again that I am not about to worship those that you worship. Nor are you about to wor-ship whom I worship. Therefore, onto you be your religion and onto me be my religion". This is the final and most deci-sive verdict of Hazrat Mohammed (PBUH) on those whom Muslims pejoratively call Kafirs, including Christians. It clearly tells Muslims not to vie with Kafirs but to live in peace and harmony with them. In other words follow the principle of mutual respect and a policy of "live and let live".

Following the verdict of their Prophet, the informed Muslims are indeed well disposed towards Christians. Christians ought to return the favor in equal measure if not more. As is well known, Muslims regard Christians as *ahl-e-Kitab* or "people of the book (i.e. people possessing God's revelation). This is a title of very high respect and honor. In a recent book—Qissis-ul-Ambia—(Life Stories of Proph-ets—a translation work by Maulana Ata-Ullah Sajid, and published by Dar-ul-Islam, Lahore) have been described the lives of some twenty-six major Judeo-Christian personages whom Muslims regard as God's "messengers"; all the way

---

[2] This refers to a state of mind where the dominant urge is to supplant other faiths rather than live with them in peace and harmony.

from Hazrat Abraham to Hazrat Issa or Jesus. It is acknowledged that Hazrat Issa was miraculously born of Virgin Mary. He possessed the power to perform miracles, even raising the dead. From the lap of his mother, as a very young child, he said of himself: "I am the servant of God. He has given me *The Book* (divine message} and made me a prophet (i.e. given me the highest rank), and made me a blessing for all people (i.e. including non-Muslims) ... From the day I was born and the day I shall die ....and the day I shall be raised from the dead, honor and blessing are mine. This is the truth, and the whole truth which has been exaggerated and manipulated by some. For it does not behoove Allah to beget a son to carry out His wishes for the sinful world. He is all-powerful. When He wills something, all He has to do is to say "become" and it becomes" (Sura Maryum, 30 -35; underlining provided).

In other words, God is so absolutely powerful that He can never be reduced to just one unattractive choice regarding the sin of man as held by Christians. Thus Hazrat Issa's death on the cross becomes a non-necessity, even a superfluity. Further, in Muslim belief, Hazrat Issa was lifted into heaven alive, and will come again at the end of time. Sura Maryum puts these words in the mouth of Hazrat Issa: "I am a man of God. He has given me the Book, and made me a prophet. Whatever circumstance I am in, He has made me a source of blessing ... And the day I was born, and the day I shall die, and the day I shall be raised from the dead, grace and peace are upon me". The Holy Qur'an continues: "This is all the truth about Mary's son Issa. But some people doubt this. Know that it is not becoming of Allah that He should create anyone as His son (just for the sake of performing a mission). Whenever He wills something, all He has to do is

151

to say 'become' and it becomes". The belief that God had to devise an awfully sadistic plan to bring universal forgiveness into operation is so much of a bunk in the Muslim way of thinking. It makes so much more sense to them to think that, if Allah wanted man's sins forgiven, all He had to do was to say: 'All your sins are forgiven etc. etc." For God is all-knowing. He must have known that man is going to continue to sin. In the light of which it may be asserted that the sacrificial death of Hazrat Issa was in vain. Sin has continued to prevail. So the question arises: How will God deal with man's post-crucifixion sins? What new expiation plan will He devise? Will there be another sacrificial lamb like Hazrat Issa? If the price of sin was paid for all time, are we now free to sin? If not, what about the post-crucifixion sin? Will the God of love and mercy have to devise another expiation plan? Christians and Muslims have their own answers to these questions.

Some Christian apologists, over the last many centuries, have been at pains to explain to Muslims that, Hazrat Issa's title as Son of God is merely an allegorical description of his and refers simply to the closeness of His relationship with God. His Sonship does not involve a literal depiction, nor does it mean any kind of physical reality. When Christians call Hazrat Issa Masih "Ib'n-e-Allah", they are merely describing, in allegorical language, the closeness of his relationship to Allah as unsurpassed by any other relationship. That is to say that, He was as close to Allah as an only son can be to his father. In fact, Hazrat Issa's own description of himself was not "son of God" but "the Son of Man" (progeny of Hazrat Adam). Some of His followers even called him "son of David" and He readily accepted that description of himself. In fact, even today Christians would really do well by their Muslim brethren to acknowledge Hazrat Issa as simply "Rooh Allah" (Spirit of God) as Muslims do. For that denotes even a much closer and essential relationship to God than the Sonship relationship. If this could happen, the overall problem will be reduced to only one dispute—His dying on the cross. There is a strong Muslim tradition that Hazrat Issa was so high in the sight of God that God could never suffer to see him die the agonizing and degrading death on the cross. The idea that God had to pay a price for the forgiveness of mankind's sins is an anathema to Muslims. They believe that God is all-powerful and all-merciful. He simply cannot be reduced to only a single option in regard to the sins of man. All He had to do was to say "become", and it would have become. That is, His mere word would have been enough to wipe out the sins of mankind. The concept of expiation, or of paying the price, is foreign to the Muslim way of thinking. According to them, it makes no sense that Allah, who is all love and all mercy and all forgiveness would stoop to extract a price for man's sins when it is so much more befitting His nature to forgive outright. In other words, the doctrine of Hazrat Issa having to die on the cross as the expiation for the sins of mankind is so much of a non-sense to Muslims as it was to His own people, the Jews; and remains to this day. It must be admitted that there is enormous appeal in the Muslim argument. The patent Christian counter argument that the loving God is also the just God, and justice requires a price to be paid for every wrong committed. The question then arises: Is God more loving and forgiving or is God more just and punishing? Christians and Muslims have different answers to this question.

In any event, the greatest Muslim dissension is regarding Hazrat Issa's death on the cross and its corollary, i.e. His rising from the dead on the third day. And they are not alone in this. Hazrat Issa's own people, the Jews, have never accepted the reality of a risen Christ. The Jewish tradition, which is the earliest, holds that Hazrat Issa was indeed tried for treason, was convicted, hung on the cross, died, and was buried in a make-shift grave. This grave was especially accessible to His close companions. So they stole his dead body, concealed it, and spread the false news that He had risen from the dead.

The tradition that was created and was strenuously promoted among His few diehard followers was that He died on the cross, was buried, but rose from the grave on the third day; ascended into heaven; now sits on the right hand of God and, in the fullness of time, will come again to judge the good and the bad. For them, the empty tomb bore proof positive of the fact of his rising.

The very plausible tradition which the Muslims follow is that, Roman soldiers stationed in Jerusalem, not knowing the precise identity of Hazrat Issa (He was admittedly an unknown figure in the city of Jerusalem and the immediately surrounding area), mistakenly arrested a man who did, or had been made to, look like Hazrat Issa, or was simply identified to them as Hazrat Issa during their arrest search for him. And thus captured and hung on the cross a common man in place of Hazrat Issa. Hazrat Issa escaped crucifixion and, in the fullness of time, was lifted into heaven. Sura Maryam, verse 15 reads: "Peace on Him the day he was born, and the day he dieth and the day he shall be raised alive". Similarly, Sura Maryam, verse 33 reads: "Peace on me the day I was born and the day I die, and the day I shall be raised alive". The story of the manner in which Hazrat Issa was arrested lends credence to the Muslim position on this matter: The Roman soldiers who were dispatched to arrest Hazrat Issa clearly did not know his identity. Obviously, as stated above, he was an obscure figure in Jerusalem and its immediate vicinity. Thus His captors needed help in identifying Him. Enter Judus, a close companion and confidant of Hazrat Issa. A scheme appears to have been worked out around him, apparently with Hazrat Issa's own consent. [Mark His words to Judas at the Last Supper (paraphrased): "Depart, and be about the task you are supposed to perform". Math. 26: 50]. Thus Judas went and brought a small dispatch of Roman soldiers to a place where Hazrat Issa and His companions were supposedly holed up, i.e. a secluded place with trees and bushes. There, in the dark of the early hours of the night, Judas misidentified to the soldiers one of the men as Hazrat Issa. Therefore, they captured a wrong man, put him through a breezy trial, where His judges too had no clue as to His precise physical identity and, after a hasty trial, ordered a wrong man to be hung on the cross. This version makes much more common sense than the highly improbable version that a loyal and devoted disciple sold away his beloved teacher and friend for a measly thirty coins; and then immediately after the completion of his faithless misdeed repented to such a degree as to kill himself over it. This story taxes credulity to a very high degree. It is far more believable that Judas actually tricked Roman soldiers into arresting someone other than Hazrat Issa. Under the circumstances, there is a fairly strong argument in the Muslim tradition that Hazrat Issa escaped capture and death, and in due time was lifted alive into heaven, from where he will come again on the Judgment Day.

But the entrenched position of Christians on this matter is what it is. It is not about to change. In the meantime, however, the only basis for rapprochement between Muslims and Christians is that either side genuinely honors the other side for its faith position. A process of reconciliation must take hold under an initiative of the Christians. In other words, Christians must recognize that Islam is good and sufficient for Muslims. They have lived with if for over thirteen hundred years without any need for change. Similarly, Muslims must recognize that Christianity is good and sufficient for Christians. They have lived with it for more than twenty centuries and have seen no need for change. In fact, there is no magical formula for change of disposition of either group toward the other. The only hope is that one side takes the initiative and continues in the change process in such a conciliatory manner that the other side finds it impossible not to respond. I hold that, in the case of Pakistan, it is the Christians who are called upon to cease this initiative. The spirit of strife should give way to the spirit of reconciliation. There is a great deal which is common to both religions. If areas of commonality are emphasized and areas of discord are pushed back into the background, the air can be cleared to a surprising degree. In this regard, the initiative lies with the Christians as, over the past centuries, it is the Christians who have arrogantly withheld due recognition from Islam and Muslims. It will be only wise of the tiny Christian minority in Pakistan to actively seek common ground with the Muslim majority, emphasize what is common to the two faiths, and push into the background those aspects where compromise appears unattainable. Thus Christians must recognize the greatness of Prophet Mohammed (PBUH) and his moral and ethical teachings. Prophet Mohammed

(PBUH) accepted the Christian tradition to a very large extent. It is a matter of great sadness that in the tradition of Christianity significant commonalities with Islam have been relegated into the background and issues of dispute have been stubbornly promoted. In any event, in the context of Pakistan, if the Christian situation is to improve, a reformed mind-set toward Islam and Muslims is an imperative.

At this point, let us digress to St. Paul's manifesto of political behavior and social morality impressed upon a tiny Christian minority in Rome of his time. In his famous letter to them, (Romans, chapter 12), he lays out the practical principles of social morality. He compares the community of believers to a human body, and the members of this community to the parts of the body. He advises each Christian to mind his own business only, without being critical of others just as the parts of the human body do towards one another. Then he lays out, in clear and specific terms, the political behavior befitting Christians. He enjoins the tiny Christian minority to obey the government of the time, asserting that there is no government that is not sanctioned by God. Therefore, he who scandalizes the established government disobeys God.

All we can say is that, when St. Paul set forth his political philosophy, the only known model of government was autocracy or kingship. The idea of democracy had not arisen then. We live today in a world where the established model of good government is democracy. The hall-mark of democracy is a balance of citizens' rights and freedoms with their duties and responsibilities. If the idea of democracy had been known in St. Paul's time, we can be certain that he would have counseled the tiny Christian minority in Rome full and robust participation in the democratic processes.

While still advocating obedience to the government of the time, he would have pressed upon Christians to faithfully participate in the socio-political processes, and to strive as creatively as possible for the protection and promotion of their personal and human rights and freedoms. Surely, he would have found this to be the will of a God who loves his people and wants them to be happy, safe, and secure in all circumstances.

In the light of this, the best counsel to the Christians of Pakistan is: Be faithful and obedient to the Government of the time. Avoid conflict at all costs. Don't be afraid of creative compromise. But, above all, develop and practice a conciliatory Christianity. This simply means that, the public face of Christian faith should be such as to cause the least friction with Islam and Muslims. Once again we recall St. Paul: "Therefore, if any one is in Christ, he is a new kind of being; the old has passed away. Behold, the new has come. All this is from God, who through Christ reconciled us to himself and gave us the ministry of reconciliation; that is, God was in Christ reconciling the world to Himself, ... and entrusted to us the message of reconciliation (2 Corinthians 5:17ff, underlining provided). Obviously, for Christians of Pakistan, the world means, first and foremost, the world of Islam and Muslims as it is found in Pakistan. A discord-oriented Christianity is bound to remain a suffocated Christianity. Only a situationally adaptive Christianity has the potential of being maximally vibrant.

This brings us to the question of a dynamic and concrete faith as opposed to a static and abstract faith. Verbal faith is good but not as good as faith with works. In my view, it is the Christianity of works which can have the most resonance with Islam, and is best suited to the Christians of

Pakistan. Islam itself is a religion of works. The five pillars of Islam are all given to concrete religious behavior, i.e. declaring faith; praying; fasting; alms giving; and pilgrimage. To be appreciated by Muslims, Christians will have to emphasize the deeds aspects of their faith rather than dwell on its verbal abstractions and high sounding theological formulations. Faith, of course, is foundational. But there must be something more than just the foundation. A material structure must rise from any foundation. Otherwise, faith alone is meaningless. If a tree has roots but bear no fruit what good are its roots? If one has faith but bears no faith-fruits, what good is his/her faith? In my view, Islam-relevant Christianity cannot but be works oriented Christianity. It must arise from a strong faith but must not be limited to just the abstract faith. Here I refer to the warning of St James issued to the Jewish-Christian minorities living here and there among people of other faiths: My brothers, he asks them, what good is faith without actions? Can such a faith alone save anyone? It is just like someone saying to a hungry person: "God bless you; stay well and eat well". What good is this if the hungry man is not helped with the act of supplying him food? St. James goes as far as to say that, mere faith without the works of faith is as good as dead. In fact, he goes on to say that faith devoid of good works is no faith at all. It simply does not exist. If one is self-satisfied with his abstract faith, one is clearly indulging in self-deception. St. James challenges such people by saying to them: "Show me (if you can), your faith without works. For faith without works is a myth (has no reality). True faith can exist only in the works of faith. Faith without works is a self-deception".

I am strongly of the view that the only faith which is viable in an Islamic environment is a faith of works. Islam is a religion of works. Muslims have no respect for a religion which is not works oriented. If Christianity is to gain the respect and honor of Muslims, it must go beyond being mere faith of words. It must become a fruit-bearing faith. In Acts 10:38 St. Peter clearly puts works above words when he asserts that the whole ministry of Hazrat Issa Masih, was based on works in that: "He went about *doing* good ...". This clearly indicates that the soul of Hazrat Issa Masih's ministry was good works. His message did not consist merely of words but the main stay of His ministry was good works repeated one after the other, without any differentiation between rich or poor, good or bad; Jew or gentile. Similarly, when St. Peter was invited by a group of non-believing inquirers to preach to them, boldly asserted: "*It is true that God treats everyone on the same basis. Whoever worships Him and does what is acceptable to Him no matter what race [or religion]) he belongs to*" is acceptable in His sight (Acts 10: 34—35). Christians have no special corner on the love of God. People of other faiths, if they worship God and "*do*" what God requires of them are equally acceptable in His sight.

Given the experience of the last many centuries, it should be clear that, the abstract and self-assuming version of Christianity has manifestly failed to make much impression on Muslims. It is my view, therefore, that what is needed in Pakistan is not West-bequeathed abstract Christianity, i.e. a Christianity abstractly oriented and intellectually theologized. But rather a Pakistani Christianity which is more deed-based; which in its form and contents, and general flavor, is more locally attuned. Ultimately, such Christianity will have to be a "humble Christianity". By this I mean a Christianity which is fully cognizant of the fact that its expressions and manifestations are a "re-constructed" version of the entire life and works of Hazrat Issa Masih by persons who had hardly any direct knowledge of him. Further, that the accounts of His life have come to us from persons who lay no claim to any heavenly "inspiration" for their narratives. It is, therefore, obvious that, they used their own re-interpretive and re-constructive imagination to build an account of Hazrat Issa Masih's life and works. Neither Mathew nor Mark, nor Luke, nor John makes a claim of having personal knowledge of Hazrat Issa Masih, or his teachings and works. A certain oral tradition about a person called Jesus had emerged among those who had seen Him perform miracles, or had heard him preach a new kind of Judaism. This is the tradition that was picked up by the Gospelers and narrated in their Gospels with their own style and selective interpretation. Like any tradition, it still remains open to the question: Did it really happen? Did a virgin really conceive? Did heaven really open at Jesus' baptism? Did Jesus actually walk on water? Did he actually feed a multitude with only five loaves? Did he actually give sight to the blind and hearing to the deaf? Or restore the dead to life? Did his own resuscitated body walk physically out of his tomb the third day after his death on the cross? Did he actually ascend into a heaven beyond the sky? It is obvious that the Gospel writers just assumed the answers to all these questions to be "yes" and left the matter at that. As Bishop Shelby Spong puts it: "So it was that the Christian Church locked itself into certain basic assumptions by which it lived and to which it admitted no challenge. Among the assumptions was that the Bible, especially the Gospels as the Word of God, were objective truth, and that, they described events of literal history, and that, therefore, one could confidently assert that all that was contained therein did in fact happen just as it was written. This mentality produced a comfortable feeling of security that endured for centuries. It was, however, destined not to endure forever."[3] (Liberating The Gospels, p. 6).

Further, a non-aggressive, or a humble Christianity, I maintain, would have to be thoroughly cognizant of the following realities: That Hazrat Issa Masih was, more than any thing else, a Jewish moral teacher. In everything, he projected nothing but his humanity. He hardly ever referred to himself as anything other than the Son of Man (Adam). He tried to prove his power by his miracles. But he was not the only one with such power. There were others in his time that performed miracles or magical acts. That he hardly ever claimed to be the Massiah. That he went about doing good like any good man of his time. That like other patriotic Jews of his time, he was preoccupied with the freedom of his people from the cruel yoke of the Romans, and even more so from the seditious power of the Jewish Sanhedrin who had sold out the freedom and honor of their people, and had become puppets of the Roman Rule over their people. That he, due to his utter anguish over the shame and degradation of his people, challenged the Roman Rule by defiantly riding into the Capital of Jerusalem with a band of his followers proclaiming him to be the king of his people. That he thus pre-maturely provoked the Roman power of the time. That they, therefore, sternly moved against him, captured him, hastily processed him, had him declared guilty of treason, and eliminated him by hanging him on a cross.

---

[3] I wish to acknowledge that I have benefitted from Bishop John Shelby Spong's two well known works listed in the bibliography

From that point on, the Jesus of history began to recede into the background and the Christ of faith began to arise in the minds and hearts of His close confidants who simply could not accept, or live with, the fact that their master/leader had been cut down so helplessly and so shamefully. That their minds went into an over-drive to find cogent rationalization for what had happened to their "master" and to their hopes and aspirations of wresting the Jewish kingdom from a foreign power by the miraculous powers of their master. But when, after his thoroughly humiliating death, every hope was dashed, the companions of the "master" went into a shell-shock. To rid themselves of the shock, they engaged in all kinds of rationalizations for all that had befallen them and their master. It is through this process that the phenomenon of his utterly humiliating death became a ransom for mankind's sins; and the "risen" Christ's ascension into heaven became a promise of his second coming at the end of time.

Obviously, the whole account of Jesus' life, i.e. his works, his death, and his rising from the dead, has come to us second hand. None of the four Gospelers had personal knowledge of Jesus who had been born as much as almost hundred years before their writing about Him (as in the case of John). The Gospel of Mark is considered to be the first written. Even that, it is universally agreed, was written some sixty-five to seventy years after the birth of Jesus by one who had no personal knowledge of the Nazarene at all. St. Luke even hints that his record is based on the hear-say accounts of others. We may, if we wish, assert that the Gospel writers were "inspired" or "God-informed" (*Irfaan*). But this would be nothing more than mere conjecture. None of the Gospelers has laid a claim to have been "inspired" by God.

Considering all this, one cannot escape the conclusion that, Christians and Christianity have a lot to be humble about.

In the end, as we take a long and hard look at the prospects for both Christianity and Christians in Pakistan, we find them to be rather problematic. The major sources of the Christian problem reside in the fundamentalist nature of Christianity, both as practiced and preached, together with the disorganization and disunity of the Christian community at almost all level of life. We have already suggested, in a limited way, some steps that should be taken in regard to the socio-political life of the community. Here we offer some brief suggestions for the religious problem of the community.

Present Christianity was brought to the Pakistan area of the Indian sub-continent more than 150 years ago. By all accounts, this Christianity was of a fundamentalist or classical kind. Thus, for its entire life, Pakistani Christianity has remained embedded in its fundamentalism bequeathed to it by the Western missionary organizations. Over the last nearly hundred years, Christianity in the West has been experiencing a phenomenal evolutionary change. The Jesus of old orthodoxy is fast being replaced by a Jesus of history and humanity. The structural foundations of faith are being violently shaken. "The Church, as it faces the beginning of its third millennium, is in crisis regarding what it believes about Jesus. Believers are in crisis about their convictions ... And the previous reconstructions of who Jesus was , what he said, and what he did are coming unraveled in the light of new information, new methodologies, and new perspectives... We should make no mistake that historical research does affect faith. The Protestant and Catholic theologians who attempted to put the convocations of faith beyond the reach of historical reconstruction and human reason have failed. The Jesus that is emerging from a re-evaluation of the ancient records in the light of new discoveries will shake the temple to its foundations". Continuing: "The quest of the historical Jesus is also about the religion to which he gave rise. The historical truth about this man may help us discover the truth about the faith he evoked. Or , conversely, the truth about the faith may open our eyes to the truth about the man. The distinction between the Jesus of history and the Jesus of the gospels and creeds threatens traditional orthodoxy and other "doxies" that constitute the formidable rampart guarding our previous convictions. But the discovery may prove to be salutary for a flabby community of faith, provided it is explored with rigor and honesty" (Robert Funk, p. 23).

If we follow this path of "exploration with rigor and honesty" we will find that it is a humbling experience. It is not too much to assert that many old formulations of Christian faith appear to be dying at the hands of modern knowledge developments. In their place, a reason-based faith is increasingly taking hold of thinking believers. In many ways the warning by Anglican Bishop Spong that, "Christianity must change or die", has begun to ring true, especially for the tiny Christian communities planted by Missions and now existing in the shadow of other religions throughout the world.

Under the circumstances, it is strongly recommend that Christians in Pakistan move away from a fundamentalist Christianity, both in content and format, and adopt a liberal or progressive Christianity. A liberal Christianity has the best chance of providing Christians of Pakistan the ability to live a life of reconciliation with Islam and Muslims. A liberal Christianity is one which is thoroughly informed by such realities as: God is not partial to anyone—Muslim, Christian, Hindu or others. He treats everyone alike whether he/she be a Jew or Gentile or anyone else. He can be worshipped in many ways and every way is acceptable in his sight. No one religion has a monopoly on God. He reveals Himself to different people in different ways and every revelation must be accepted on its own terms. Surely God can be conceived and worshipped in many ways and forms. That, while one may belong to a particular religious tradition, he/she does not give up the right to relate to God in his/her personal way. Therefore, everyone has the inalienable right to worship God in his own way. That, if one has a personal relationship with God, one ought to be at liberty to have a personal view of God. That, since ultimately salvation is personal, the ways of salvation must also be personal. That the views of heaven and hell, good or bad, right or wrong are culture-bound and, therefore, continue to evolve with culture. Cultural evolution is continuous and so is religious evolution. Consequently, none should be bound by a fixed view of good or bad, heaven or hell, sin or righteousness.

That the Scriptures, though they contain the divine message, have come to us through the agency of fallible human beings and, therefore, remain subject to human error. Man's search for truth has not come to an end. It is an ongoing task rather than something that has been accomplished. This search must continue. It is therefore that Christianity must adopt the humble attitude recommended by St. Paul—"For now we see though a (fogy) glass rather dimly. But a time will come when we will see the truth face to face. Now our knowledge is partial but a time will come when we will know

God more completely as He knows us completely" (1 Corinthians, 13:12).

The quality of Christian-Muslim relations in Pakistan, as in any situation of inter-communal relations, will always depend upon the degree of mutuality between Christians and Muslims, i.e. greater the mutuality smoother the relationships. Or, conversely: higher the mutual exclusion more difficult the relationships. Therefore, the central goal of the Christian minority must be to bring about the highest degree of mutuality between themselves and their Muslim neighbors. This will not be possible so long as Christians continue to have a kind of chip on their shoulder. Every religion is good and complete in the sight of its adherers. Others must accept this fact at its face value. Certainly Christians have a right to consider their own religion as more perfect. But, by the same token, Muslims have as much right to consider their religion as more perfect. Therefore, missionism, as such, must go out of the window and a true spirit of accommodation must come to prevail. This, however, will not be possible unless a "local" Christianity, or more properly, a "contextual" Christianity comes to prevail. I refrain from suggesting the details of a contextual Christianity for Pakistan. I consign this crucial task of developing a suitable contextual Christianity to the Christian community of Pakistan. Only they know the true nature of their context. Only they can know the true contingencies that must be dealt with, and the price that must be paid for a rapprochement and reconciliation with the Islamic environment in which they are destined to live.

My last plea to the Christians of Pakistan is: Practice a living religion. Christianity is indeed a living religion. It is in the nature of living things to continuously evolve. The key to successful evolution is perpetual adaptation to the environment. The Islamic environment of Pakistan is something to adapt to, not something to be at odds with. Follow a Christianity which is more of the head than of the heart. Change your mind-set toward Muslims. Abandon traditional negativity toward Islam. Seek positive integration into the Islamic socio-cultural milieu. Become an essential part of it. At every step, seek reconciliation and integration. Develop a whole-hearted identification with Pakistan. It is the land of your ancestors and of your future generations to come. Stand by your human rights and freedoms with quiet persistence and Christian humility. If God is truly your shepherd, He will be by you at all times, in all situations, and in every way. If minority living is your lot, accept it with grace without being broken by it.

APPENDIX A
Umar's Pact
(The Status of Non-Muslims)

This is a general draft of a pact of zimmitude (ward-ship) for Christians under Muslim rule proposed to Khalifa Umar 11 (717- 720) and his enthusiastic endorsement of it:

"This is a letter to the servant of God Umar, commander of the faithful, from the Christians of such and such city. When you came against us, we asked you for safe–conduct (aman) for ourselves, our dependents, our property, and the people of our community, and we undertook the following obligations towards you: We shall not build, in our cities or in the neighborhoods, new monasteries, churches, convents, or monk's cells, nor shall we repair, by day or by night, such of them as fall in ruins or are situated in the quarters of the Muslims. We shall keep our gates wide open for passersby and travelers. We shall give board and lodging to all Muslims who pass our way for three days. We shall not give shelter in our churches or in any other dwelling to any spy, nor hide him from the Muslims. We shall not teach the Qur'an to our children. We shall not manifest our religion publicly nor convert anyone to it. We shall not prevent any of our kin from entering Islam if they wish it. We shall show respect towards the Muslims, and we shall rise from our seats when they wish to sit. We shall not seek to resemble the Muslims by imitating any of their garments, the qulansuwa, the turban, footwear, or the parting of the hair. We shall not speak as they do, nor shall we adopt their kunyas [i.e. names starting with "Abu" for father, or "Umm" for mother]. We shall not mount on saddles nor shall we gird our swords nor bear any kind of arms nor carry them on our persons. We shall not engrave Arabic inscriptions on our seals. We shall not sell fermented drinks. We shall clip the fronts of our heads. We shall always dress in the same way wherever we may be, and we shall bind the "zunar" round our waists. We shall not display our crosses or our books in the roads or the markets of the Muslims. We shall use only clappers in our churches very softly. We shall not raise our voices when following our dead. We shall not show lights on any of the roads of the Muslims or in their markets. We shall not bury our dead near the Muslims. We shall not take slaves who have been allotted to the Muslims. We shall not build houses taller than the houses of the Muslims. We shall not strike a Muslim. We accept these conditions for ourselves and the people of our community, and in return we receive safe-conduct. If we in any way violate these undertakings for which we ourselves stand surety, we forfeit our covenant [zimmah] and we become liable to the penalties for contumacy and sedition."

In response, Umar ibn al-Khittab ordered to have the pact signed with two additions: Christians shall not buy any one made prisoner by the Muslims; and whosoever shall strike a Muslim with deliberate intent shall forfeit the protection of the Pact.

APPENDIX B

The Objectives Resolution
(Pakistan Constitution Article 2A)

Whereas sovereignty over the entire universe belongs to Allah Almighty alone and the authority which He has delegated to the State of Pakistan through its people for being exercised within the limits prescribed by Him is a sacred trust;

This Constituent Assembly representing the people of Pakistan resolves to frame a Constitution for the sovereign independent State of Pakistan;

Wherein the State shall exercise its powers and authority through the chosen representatives of the people;

Wherein the principles of democracy, freedom, equality, tolerance and social justice as enunciated by Islam shall be fully observed;

Wherein the Muslims shall be enabled to order their lives in the individual and collective spheres in accordance with the teachings and requirements of Islam as set out in the Holy Quran and the Sunnah;

Wherein adequate provision shall be made for the minorities to profess and practice their religions and develop their cultures;

Wherein the territories now included in or in accession with Pakistan and such other territories as may be included in or accede to Pakistan shall form a Federation wherein the units will be autonomous with such boundaries and limitations on their powers and authority as may be prescribed;

Wherein shall be guaranteed fundamental rights including equality of status, of opportunity and before law, social, economic and political justice, and freedom of thought, expression, belief, worship and association, subject to the Law and public morality;

Wherein adequate provision shall be made to safeguard the legitimate interests of the minorities and backward and depressed classes;

Wherein the independence of the judiciary shall be fully secured;

Wherein the integrity of the territories of the Federation, its independence and all its rights including its sovereign right on land, sea and air shall be safeguarded;

So that the people of Pakistan may prosper and attain their rightful and honored place amongst the nations of the world and make their full contribution towards international peace and progress and happiness of humanity.

APPENDIX C
Blasphemy and Related Islamic Laws

Injuring or defiling places of worship, with intent to insult the religion of any class: Whoever, destroys, damages or defiles any place of worship, or any object held sacred by any class of persons with the intention of thereby insulting the religion of any class of persons or with the knowledge that any class of persons is likely to consider such destruction, damage or defilement as an insult to their religion, shall be punished with imprisonment of either description for a term which may extend to two years, or with fine, or with both.

Section 295-A

Deliberate and malicious acts intended to outrage religious feelings of any class by insulting its religion or religious beliefs: Whoever with deliberate and malicious intention of outraging the religious feelings of any class of the citizens of Pakistan by words, either spoken or written or representa-

APPENDIX C

tion, insults or attempts to insult the religion or the religious beliefs of that class, shall be punished with imprisonment of either description for a term which may extend to ten years, or with fine, or with both.

Blasphemy Laws:

Section 295-B

Defiling, etc., of copy of the Holy Qur'an : Whoever willfully defiles, damages or desecrates a copy of the Holy Qur'an or an extract therefrom or uses it in any derogatory manner or for any unlawful purpose shall be punishable with imprisonment for life.

Section 295-C

Use of derogatory remarks etc., in respect of the Holy Prophet: Whoever by word, either spoken or written or by visible representation, or by any imputation, innuendo, or insinuation, directly or indirectly, defiles the sacred name of the Holy Prophet Mohammed (peace be upon him) shall be punished with death.

Section 298

Uttering words, etc., with deliberate intent of wounding religious feelings: Whoever, wit deliberate intention of wounding the religious feelings of any person utters a words or makes any sound in the hearing of that person or makes any gesture in the sights of that person or places any object in the sights of that person, shall be punished with imprisonment or either description for a term which may extend to one year, or with fine, or with both.

Use of derogatory remarks etc., in respect of holy personages: Whoever by word, either spoken or written, or by visible representation, or by imputation, innuendo or insinuation, directly or indirectly, defiles the sacred name of any wife (Ummul Mumineen), or members of the family (Ahle-bait), of the Holy Prophet (peace be upon him), or any of the righteous Caliphs (Khulafa-e-Raashideen) or companions (Sahaaba) of the Holy Prophet (peace be upon him) shall be punished with imprisonment of either description for a term which may extend to three years, or with fine, or with both.

Section 298-B

Misuse of epithets, description and title, etc., reserved for certain holy personages or places: (1) Any person of the Qadiani group or the Lahori group (who call themselves "Ahmadis" or by any other name) who by words, either spoken or written, or by visible representation: (a) refer to, or addresses, any person, other than a Caliph or companion of the Holy Prophet Muhammad (peace be upon him), as "Ameer-ul-Mumineen", Khalifat-ul-Mumineen", "Khalifat-ul-Muslimeen", "Sahaabi" or "Razi Allah Anho"; (b) Refers to, or addresses, any person, other than a wife of the Holy Prophet Muhammad (peace be upon him), as Ummal-Mumineen; (c) refers to, or addresses, any person, other than a member of the family (Ahle-bait) of the Holy Prophet Muhammad (peace be upon him), as Ahle-bait; or (d) refers to, or names, or calls, his place of worship as Masjid (mosque); shall be punished with imprisonment of either description for a term which may extend to three years, and shall be also liable for fine. (2) Any person of the Qadiani group or Lahori group (who call themselves "Ahmadis" or by any other name) who by words, either spoken or written, or by visible representation, refers to the mode or form of call to prayers followed by his faith as "Azan" or recite Azan as used by the Muslims, shall be punished with imprisonment of either description for a term which may extend to three years and shall also be liable to fine.

Section 298-C

Persons of Qadiani group, etc., calling himself a Muslim or preaching or propagating his faith: A person of the of the Qadiani group or the Lahori group (who call themselves "Ahmadis" or by any other name), who, directly or indirectly, pose himself as a Muslim, or calls, or refers to, his faith as Islam, or preaches or propagates his faith, or invites others to accept his faith, by word, either spoken or written, or by visible representation or in any other manner whatsoever outrages the religious feelings of Muslims, shall be punished with imprisonment of either description for term which may extend to three years and shall also be liable to fine.

BIBLIOGRAPHY

Anderson, W. L. *One Hundred Years of Christian Work,* Mysore, India, Wesley Press, 1940

Bolitho, H. *Jinnah, Creator of Pakistan,* Berkeley, University of California Press, 1961

Blunt, W. S. *"The Mohammedan Question",* Fortnightly Review, XLIV, (November, 1884)

Brown, L. E. *The Great Muslim Wall,* Westminster, Society for the Propagation of the Gospel , 1931

Clark, Robert. *The Punjab and Sind Missions of the Church Missionary Society,* London, 1885

Cumming, Sir John (ed) *Political India 1823—1932*, Oxford University Press, 1932

Funk, Robert. *Honest to Jesus,* New York, HarperCollins, 1996

Gordon, Andrew. *Our India Mission,* Philadelphia, the author, 1886

Gallard, Keith. *Pakistan, A Political Study,* London, Allen and Erwin Ltd., 1957

Hutton, L. H. *Castes in India,* 3rd. ed. Oxford University Press, 1961

BIBLIOGRAPHY

Herrick, C.F. *Christian and Mohammedan,* New York, Fleming H. Revell, 1912

Ibbetson (Sir) Denzil. *Punjab Tribes and Castes,* Lahore, Government Printing Press, 1883

Levonian, L. *Muslim Mentality,* London, George Allen and Urwin, 1928

Lowrie, J.C. *Two Years in Upper India,* New York, R. Carter and Brothers, 1850

Mayhew, Arthur. *Christianity and the Government of India,* Faber and Gwyer Ltd. 1919

Ogilvie, J.N. *Our Empire's Debt to Missions,* London, Hodder and Stroughton Ltd. 1924

Picket, w. *Christian Mass Movements in India,* New York, Abingdon Press, 1933

Pratt, J.B. *India and its Faiths,* New York, Houghton, 1915

Richter, Julius. *A History of Missions in India,* Fleming H. Revell & Co, 1908

Rose, Horace Arthur. *A Glossary of the Tribes and Castes of the Punjab,* Lahore, Government Printing Press, 1911

Risley, (Sir) Herbert. *The People of India,* Calcutta, Thaker, Spink & Co. 1915

Stewart, Robert. *Life and Work in India,* Philadelphia, Pearl Publishing Co., 1899

Smith, W, Cantwell. *Modern Islam in India,* Lahore, Minerva Book Shop, 1943

Smith, Morton. *Jesus The Magician, Charlatan or Son of God,* San Francisco, Harper & Row, 1978

Spong, John Shelby. *Liberating the Gospels*, San Francisco, Harper, 1996

--------------------*Why Christianity Must Change or Die,* Harper-Collins, 1988

Stock, E. *The History of the Church Missionary Society,* London, 1899

Symond, Richard. *Making of Pakistan,* London, Faber and Faber, 1950

Taylor, N.F.L.. *Our Punjab Mission,* Edinburgh, Church of Scotland, 1840

Thompson, Edward and Garratt, G.T. *The Rise and Fulfillment of the British Rule in India,* London, Macmillan and Co, 1934

Williams, Rushbrook. *The State of Pakistan,* London, Faber and Faber, 1962

OFFICIAL PUBLICATIONS

The Constitution of Pakistan 1956. Karachi, Government of Pakistan, Department of Advertising, Films and Publications, 1956

The Constitution of Pakistan 1961. Karachi, Government of Pakistan Press, 1962

The Constitution of Pakistan 1973. Kausar Brothers, Law Book Publishers, Lahore

Lightning Source UK Ltd.
Milton Keynes UK
11 June 2010